Seeking PEACE

True stories of Mennonites around the world, struggling to *live* their belief in peace. Full of courage and spirit!

Titus Peachey
and
Linda Gehman Peachey

Good Books

Intercourse, PA 17534

Design by Dawn J. Ranck
Cover design by Cheryl Benner

SEEKING PEACE
Copyright © 1991 by Good Books, Intercourse, PA 17534
International Standard Book Number: 1-56148-049-5
Library of Congress Catalog Card Number: 91-74053

**Library of Congress Cataloging-in-Publication Data is available from
the publisher upon request.**

Table of Contents

About This Book

Welcome. In the pages of this book you will meet people who have embarked on a journey toward peace.

These are ordinary folks from around the world who belong to the Anabaptist family of Christians, including Mennonites, Amish, Hutterian Brethren and the Brethren in Christ. Seeking to follow Jesus, they struggle to live out the truth that God loves all people, even the "enemy." This teaching is particularly evident in Jesus' Sermon on the Mount (Gospel of Matthew, chapters 5-7) and his choice to accept death on a cross rather than defend himself or seek vengeance. The Anabaptists believe that followers of Christ must not take the life of another human being, even if it means losing one's own life.

The stories in this book struggle with some of the many practical concerns related to this central conviction. The reader will find stories about serving in the military, paying taxes for war, working on military contracts, finding personal safety, and relating to the "enemy." Larger and deeper questions are always present. What happens if one's faith conflicts with loyalty to family and country? How will following Christ's way of peace affect desires for economic well-being, security, and social acceptance?

The majority of stories are contemporary. Yet they are all rooted in the history of the Anabaptist movement which arose in the midst of the Protestant Reformation. Sixteenth century Anabaptists emphasized the need for every Christian to claim Jesus as Lord, and to follow Jesus' teaching and example in all aspects of daily life. There was no division between clergy and laity, between private and public life. Adult baptism, nonresistant love, loyalty to the Kingdom of God, faithful discipleship and evangelism became central concerns.

These Anabaptist peoples now number nearly one million members and come from some sixty countries worldwide. For a fuller description of the history and thinking of the Anabaptist movement, we invite the reader to turn to the sources listed in the bibliography at the end of this book.

Anabaptist people do not always agree on all applications of peacemaking. Thus, the reader will find some diversity of perspective in these stories. These stories are intended to represent sincerity of conviction rather than uniformity of practice.

While this collection of stories is limited to the Anabaptist family, we recognize with gratitude the many stories of faith from other traditions which have nurtured our own commitment to Christ's way of peace.

We also want to acknowledge that many Christians do not share the convictions found in the pages of this book. The stories gathered here are not intended as an argument, but rather as the witness of a people who have sought to follow Christ's way of peace, and who have sometimes failed.

The primary focus of this book is the question of war and preparations for it. Nevertheless, the ethic of suffering love demonstrated in the life of Jesus extends to all of life. When faithfully lived, it permeates family life and relationships with neighbors. It speaks to how we handle conflict in our church life and business dealings. It influences how tightly we hold to our possessions when threatened with personal violence or harm. Thus, there is still much to learn about following Christ.

Let us help one another on this journey toward peace.

The Man Who Would Not Shoot

Mennonite young men in the Southern states had few good options at the beginning of the American Civil War, since there were no legal provisions for conscientious objectors (COs). Some of these young Mennonites chose to migrate secretly to the North or hide out in the hills and woods rather than take up arms in violation of their convictions. While an 1862 Confederate Government bill provided that conscientious objectors could hire substitutes, pay a $500 tax or serve as noncombatants, exemptions became more and more difficult to procure as the situation in the South worsened.[1] In this context, Christian and Daniel Good, two Mennonite youth from Harrisonburg, Virginia, were drafted into the Confederate Army, and struggled with their convictions against the taking of human life.

Christian and Daniel Good were drafted early during the Civil War. They were sons of a widowed mother, and almost the sole means of support for her and a number of their younger siblings. Their appeals for release were not heeded by the officials and both sons were sent to the military camp at Winchester, Virginia, where they remained during the winter of 1861 and 1862. Daniel found his way home and later tried to flee to the North with sixty or seventy others who posed as refugees. They were all captured and carried to prison at Richmond, Virginia.

Christian remained at the military camp. With the opening of the military campaign against Harpers Ferry, West Virginia, he found himself out on the firing line. When the officer in charge gave the order to shoot, Christian and several others refused. Christian was the first to be discovered and was called to appear before the officer for questioning.

"Did you shoot when you were commanded to shoot?" demanded the officer.

Christian replied, "No, I didn't see anything to shoot at."

The officer continued, "Didn't you see all those Yankees over there?"

"No, they're people," answered Christian. "We don't shoot people."[2]

The officer ordered Christian back to his place, and threatened to have Christian court-martialed and shot if the offense was repeated. Christian continued to refuse to fire and gained the nickname among the members of his company as "the man who would not shoot."

Because of this firm stand, other Mennonite young men also withheld their fire, and were jokingly referred to by their comrades as the boys whose guns were "out of order." When questioned again, Christian boldly replied that his gun never would be fired at his fellowman, even if it cost his own life. He explained that he had left a widowed mother at home who expected him to keep a sacred pledge that forbade him to fire a gun at any other person.

The officer broke into a hearty laugh, and in short order assigned the group of COs to drive horse teams. They performed this noncombatant duty during the rest of the campaign of 1862, when the Southern army retreated southward through the Shenandoah Valley.[3]

Brackets for Turret Guns

In 1941, Richard Ross was working as a machinist at the West-
inghouse Corporation in Lima, Ohio, making $120 to $130 per week.
On this income, he and his wife were able to tithe and still easily bank
$70 dollars each week. The entry of the United States into World War
II, however, was about to change his life.

I was not yet fully aware that Westinghouse was gearing up to
produce military materials, and the war rumors were negli-
gible. However, the draft was in full swing, and we who were
conscientious objectors (COs) were looking at alternate service
possibilities. Some friends of mine had already been drafted.

There were approximately twelve Mennonites working at Westinghouse when Pearl Harbor was bombed. I was operating a lathe when
an associate came back from a break and informed me of the
bombing. We were all stunned, and operations ceased as we
gathered in small groups to talk about this new threat.

For those of us who were COs, the news caused additional alarm,
as we could begin to imagine what this might mean to us if
Westinghouse were to become engaged in producing war material.
I was very certain what I would do. I could not, in good conscience,
aid in producing any materials which would in any way be used to
maim or kill. I knew I would be ready to make any sacrifice
necessary to retain my strong convictions against war.

Before long, I came to realize that the new steel brackets I was
machining were the end brackets for electronically controlled mo-
tors, to be used to turn turret guns on flying bombers. At about the
same time, I was being asked to work on Sundays, which I refused
to do, also as a matter of conscience.

Two weeks after our first child was born, I resigned from my job,
the first CO to do so at Westinghouse in Lima. My resignation card,
filed in the office by a niece of mine who was not Mennonite, stated
"re-hire anytime."

I left Westinghouse and took a job at a carburetor re-building company, making $15 per week. Six weeks later I was able to secure a position as an automotive machinist, where I began at $30 per week, with only small increases throughout the duration of the war. We continued to tithe, and to place small amounts in savings each week.

I have never regretted my decision to live up to my convictions. I believe faithfulness to God in these areas laid a faith-basis for obedience to God's call to ministry in subsequent years. I have been richly fulfilled in ministry, and adequately provided for monetarily. I am grateful for faithful teachers and preachers who stirred conviction in my life, in areas vital to following Christ and his way of peace.[1]

The Conscription of Oscar Zepeda

In 1984, seventeen-year-old Oscar Zepeda had a problem. His conscience would not allow him to participate in war, yet he lived in a country which was being torn apart by a brutal civil war—a war whose weapons were supplied primarily by the United States and the Soviet Union.

Oscar is a Mennonite in Nicaragua, and shortly after the Sandinistas instituted military conscription to fight the war against the Contras, Oscar was called before his local draft board. Accompanied by his mother, Oscar told the board that as a Christian he could not kill or participate in warfare. He was given a medical examination, and the doctors found that Oscar was flat-footed. Nonetheless, he was ordered to return in three days to leave for military training.

On the spot, Oscar volunteered to serve his country for four years without pay rather than join the military. He repeated that going to the mountains to fight would be a violation of his conscience. The draft board asked Oscar if his church required this of him, or if his conviction came from his own conscience. Oscar indicated that this was a personal matter for him, and repeated that he would not appear for his next appointment.

On the day of his appointment for military training, Oscar remained at home. After midnight, two policemen and an internal security guard knocked on the door of his home and asked him to go with them to the police station. His parents accompanied him to the station but were not permitted to go with him to the military training center. They urged Oscar to confide in God, and promised to seek his release.

Oscar was taken to a military camp where all those who refused induction were taken for thirty days of orientation. For the next month, Oscar was repeatedly requested to join the military. "Is the evangelical ready now?" they would ask.

Over twenty young men were held at the training center. Oscar and others sang songs and choruses together, but the officials were disturbed by this behavior and took their guitars away. The officials blamed Oscar for creating a disturbance, and for inciting a negative attitude toward the military. They called him a devil, and threatened him.

Oscar remained firm, and restated his conviction that peace could not come to Nicaragua through warfare. The military officials told Oscar in response that he was useless to them, and that his attitude would make him a liability in the mountains. It would be best, they told him, if they just shot him and buried him in the swamp. That would save them the expense of a casket and a funeral.

Oscar told the officials that he was not afraid to die—rather, he was afraid to kill another person. The officials told him that he was stubborn, and he should prepare to go to the mountains in three days.

Oscar's parents and the parents of his friends at the training center came to say goodbye before the group departed for the mountains. His family's appeals to the officials for his release were again ignored. "Where is God?" Oscar wondered. All human resources had failed. Oscar concluded that he needed to put his faith in God, and not in human effort. He got a strange feeling that he would soon be returning home.

The next day, Oscar and the others boarded six trucks for the two-day journey to a training camp along the Nicaragua-Honduras border. Oscar had refused military clothing, and he suffered from the cold and rain. Others shared their jackets with him.

On the first day at this camp, Oscar was examined by a physician, and due to his flat feet, was declared unfit for military service. He was released within three hours. When he arrived, he found his parents, the pastor and others gathered in prayer on his behalf.

At no time during his military experience was Oscar physically harmed. He faced constant psychological pressure, however, and feared that he would sacrifice his testimony. Throughout the thirty days he resisted wearing a uniform and did not carry a gun.

Oscar notes that several factors helped him to remain strong. The prayers of his parents, his pastor and the church were important. He also felt he was ready to die if necessary, and therefore was able to express his convictions with firmness at each turn of events. Finally, the testimony of his life, and the work of his church in his home community, resulted in more lenient treatment.

Since this experience, the draft board has recalled Oscar four times, each time thoroughly reviewing his case, asking Oscar if he still holds the same convictions about military service. Now, however, Oscar has been placed on a reserve list, and if he is called before the board, there are few questions.

Friday Will Be Peace Day

During the 1991 war in the Persian Gulf, Americans in every town and community sought ways to show their support for the troops and their loyalty to America. This was especially true in the public schools. Special assemblies were held to hear presentations from military personnel. School children wrote letters to the soldiers, made flags and yellow ribbons, and collected foot powder to send to the troops.

In this context, teachers who believed that war is contradictory to Christ's way of peace often felt isolated from their colleagues and estranged from their surroundings. One community's Mennonite Commission on Education scheduled two meetings to provide a forum for teachers to share their experiences and support one another. The story below represents one teacher's* attempt to respond to the expectations of the school, yet still be faithful to her beliefs.

**Friday will be Peace Day.
Everyone wear red, white
and blue. Each classroom
supply a bit of yellow.**

The memo from the school office made me nervous. How could I respond to this directive and remain true to my commitment as a Christian peacemaker? After much thought and prayer, and with encouragement from the Commission on Education meeting with teachers, I chose not to dress in red, white and blue.

However, I knew I needed to supply my first graders with that 'bit of yellow.'

On Peace Day I asked my class, "What is peace? How do we get it? What would make peace in this war?"

*This story is shared anonymously by request

In chorus the class responded, "Stop fighting!" Then I introduced the dove as a symbol for peace. We decided to make yellow peace doves to wear, to show that we wanted peace.

In groups of three, we started our cooperative learning project. Each group had one yellow paper, one dove pattern, one pair of scissors and a pencil. Before they began to trace and cut, they were to decide on a "peace plan"—how they would work together to make their peace doves.

At the end of the work time each group shared its "peace plan" and how they decided to cooperate to make their doves. Taking turns, polite suggestions and happy talk were parts of these "peace plans."

What was the school's response? No one asked me why I didn't wear red, white and blue. I think they already knew. People did ask my children what they were wearing. Their answers echoed, "A peace bird—to stop the war!"[1]

Bombies and Armed Escorts

Titus and Linda Peachey (authors of this book) directed the Mennonite Central Committee relief and development program in the country of Laos from 1981-1985. Heavily bombed by the United States during the Indo-China War, Laos was still suffering from the war's long-term impact. As Titus and Linda traveled throughout the countryside, they met many villagers who had survived the bombing.

We were privileged to be part of the first post-war trip made by relief agencies (Quakers, Mennonites and U.N. agencies) to the province of Houa Phan. The headquarters of the revolutionary forces during the war, Houa Phan had been very heavily bombed.

We were graciously received by people who had endured tremendous hardship. Some villagers had lived in caves for nine years. Schools and health clinics had been held in caves for reasons of safety. Villagers spoke of planting their rice at nighttime, then hurrying back to the caves before dawn and the continuation of bombing.

One of the more memorable moments for us was a cultural presentation at a public auditorium in Sam Neua, the province capital. Local groups sang and performed Lao dances for our visiting delegation. When, as is the custom in Laos, the guests were asked to respond in some way, our delegation of Americans, Germans, Poles, Nepalis, and Lao turned to the two Mennonites to sing a song. We sang a song about peace, "Last night I had the strangest dream—I dreamed the world had all agreed to put an end to war."

Our listeners received the song warmly, but with a sense of genuine surprise. "This is wonderful to have Americans come to Sam Neua and sing about peace. During the war, all we knew about America was that it was the country which bombed us and made war against us. We didn't know why. To hear you sing about peace makes us very happy. It is historic!"

Some of those who heard the song had obviously caught a radically new glimpse of Americans. And we received a painful new image of ourselves: representatives of a country far away which showed itself to lamp-lit peasant villages in the form of bombs and fighter aircraft. We were to see this image of ourselves hundreds of times throughout the five years we lived in Laos.

Linda still recalls her first trip to Xieng Khouang, another province that had been heavily bombed by American planes during the war: "As we flew over these plains, we could clearly see hundreds of bomb craters scattered over the rice fields. A day after our delegation arrived, a woman was killed by a small anti-personnel cluster 'bombie' which had lain buried in the ground since the war. Having just moved to the area, she was hoeing a new garden in which to grow some vegetables for her husband and eleven children. Her hoe hit the bombie, causing it to explode.

"The province leadership took us to visit the family. They did not dare to call us Americans, but introduced us simply as United Nations personnel. Although we felt uncomfortable, like intruders, the family was quite eager to talk to us and explain what had happened. They even gave us the hoe head that had been shattered by the bombie. 'Tell others what has happened here,' they said, hoping to bring some meaning out of the faceless violence which had claimed their wife and mother."

The cluster bomb issue began a deep stirring in our bones around the questions of guilt, responsibility and the meaning of God's peace. Each time we visited Xieng Khouang Province and attempted to help the Lao deal with these leftover cluster bombs, we had to confront a part of our American legacy which continued to threaten our Lao friends as they went about the daily tasks of living.

We heard repeated stories of injury or death from cluster bombs. In addition to these stories of pain, we were also confronted by the empty cluster bomb containers. The containers were everywhere, used as fence posts, as planters for herbs and spices, as pillars for houses or feed troughs for animals. Some containers still bore the name and address of the U.S. company which had manufactured them—American cities and towns which we knew, mirrors of our prosperity, our creative energy and our sin.

Never did Lao villagers hold us personally accountable for the terror which had befallen them, yet we could not escape the strong implication of complicity. It hung in the air—especially as we watched our friend Boua Van carefully carry bombies from a field with his bare hands. Boua Van had a passion for ridding Xieng Khouang Province of this terror.

Our connection to the violence which lay in Lao fields and gardens did not fade with our return to the United States. One winter day in the Philadelphia Free Library, while Titus was researching the current U.S. production of cluster bombs, his eye fell upon a photo news item in an issue of *Aviation Week and Space Technology*[1] magazine. Titled "Cluster Bomb Has Programmable Option," the photo displayed a new type of cluster bomb developed for export by ISC Technologies Inc., of Lancaster, Pennsylvania. He says, "I was shocked and enraged by the presence of a cluster bomb manufacturer in Lancaster, Pennsylvania, one of the largest Mennonite, Amish and Brethren in Christ communities in North America. Lancaster County was also the home of Mennonite Central Committee. Would our efforts to help Lao farmers safely dispose of cluster bombs have any integrity if we were silent about this production in our Mennonite communities?

"The Lancaster newspapers publicly lauded ISC and its contribution to the local community. Located in a well-tended industrial park, it represented prosperity, normalcy, and respectability. There were no maimed bodies to see. It was the ultimate in camouflage—a scandalous lie and an affront to our many acquaintances in Laos whose lives had been forever changed by the deadly bombs in their fields."

We were troubled by the direct connections between our American economic life and the dangers experienced by Lao villagers. Knowing that we could not live in ways which were completely pure and free from war-making, we nonetheless determined to pay as few war taxes as possible. Today we live on a reduced income in order to limit our federal tax liability. If we still owe federal taxes at the end of the year, we decline to pay the military portion and give it to a worthy charitable cause.

By considerably reducing the amount of war taxes we must pay, we seek a relationship of integrity with God and with the worldwide church. We cannot keep in our minds the picture of Mr. Boua Van carrying bombies from a field, pray for his safety, and continue to pay all of our war taxes. The contradiction is too great.

The struggle is not easy, and we have often been inconsistent. Titus remembers an incident in Laos which still troubles him today:

"Whenever we traveled in Laos, our Lao government counterparts were responsible for our food, accommodations and transportation, normally providing an armed escort to travel with us. This was a matter of protocol and proper treatment for foreign guests. We tolerated the armed escort because security was not a genuine concern. The escorts were a handy extra pair of hands to help carry supplies, remove obstructing trees from the road or pick coconuts from treetops for a refreshing drink of coconut milk.

"On one occasion, as I prepared for a one-day trip to a district hospital in one of the southern provinces, I was astounded to see four Lao soldiers on the back of our pickup, armed with machine guns and grenade launchers. I was in a quandary. This was not consistent with my image of myself, or my commitment to Christ and the way of the cross. I found myself wishing that we had raised this concern with Lao officials earlier.

"I really wanted to make the trip, since I had not visited the area before, and it was an area where the Christian church was particularly strong. I decided to go, and except for the fact that I became desperately ill with high fever, diarrhea and vomiting, the trip was uneventful.

"As I look back on the experience, I am disappointed by my lack of courage. Had any of the young soldiers been killed, or killed others in defense of my life, I would have been devastated. But my dilemma on that day in Laos was only a highly focused version of the dilemma which all American Christians face daily. We too are protected by 'armed escorts' in the form of the U.S. military which has the world's most massive and deadly arsenal of weapons. Unlike this one experience in Laos, we must live with the fact that our armed escorts do kill blatantly and openly, in order to protect us and our standard of living. In light of this, our personal adjustment in income level and our commitment to resist the payment of war taxes, seem timid and inadequate."

Laos has forever changed us. There we began to view the world from the perspective of those who have suffered from war, poverty and oppression. Today we are left with a nagging question: "Is it possible to live out the meaning of Christ's way of peace and live as citizens of a violent superpower?" We hope so, but we are witnesses to the fact that it is a great struggle, and we are only at the beginning.

Building Bridges,
Building Hope

Wilson Ogwada is an active participant in the Kenya Mennonite Church and a government official living in the Ogwedhi-Sigawa region. The area is inhabited by both Luo and Maasai peoples, two groups historically hostile to each other. The road in the center of the Ogwedhi market marks the boundary between the two tribes.

The Maasai have long been a proud, warrior people who once ruled much of East Africa. Believing that God created cattle especially for them, they have had few scruples about raiding other tribes for cattle. Today, they continue to be a wealthy people, grazing large herds of cattle on open tracts of land. Rejecting Western influences and education in favor of their own culture, they are often viewed as pagan and primitive by their neighbors.

The Luo, by contrast, are farmers and have much more readily adopted Western education and religion. With fewer resources and a larger population on their available land, they also tend to be much poorer. Often, the Luo end up sharecropping on Maasai land.

Tension over land and cattle raids has often led to violence between the two groups. In the mid-1970s, such unrest resulted in the deaths of more than fifty people. Government leaders then met with local tribal leaders from both sides to discuss the situation. As one of the local government officials, Wilson Ogwada participated in those meetings.

At the meetings we decided that we would like to invite a church to start a development project on the border to try and get the two sides working together, to help bring peace. The Maasai volunteered to donate a tract of land for the project. The group asked me to find a church to work with the center.

"So I took the idea to Zedekiah Kisare, the Bishop of the Kenya

Mennonite church. At first he was reluctant, saying that the Maasai have been our enemies for a long time and they might kill our people if we sent them there. After more discussion, he agreed that we should take this opportunity to help the Maasai.

"Since most of our church people are of the Luo tribe we felt it was important that we have a missionary family be a part of the team. We were happy when Eastern Mennonite Board (Salunga, Pennsylvania) appointed Leon and LouAnn Ressler. The Kenya Mennonite Church appointed Paul Otieno to be the evangelist and church leader. We formed a management team with nine voting members: three chosen by the Kenya Mennonite Church, three chosen by the Maasai and three chosen by the Luo community. Local government officials sit on the committee as advisors and I have served on the committee in that capacity from the beginning.

"One of our goals for the project was to open a primary school for the children in our area. If the children from these two groups can study and play together, as they grow older they will become friends and old animosities will fade away.

"Another major goal was to improve the productivity of farmers in our area. We have been suffering with the cycles of famine in Africa—one of the many reasons for that is the low productivity on many of our small African farms. Many farmers are only producing twenty-five to fifty percent of their potential."

One of the Maasai participants notes that more efficient agricultural methods are crucial: "We Maasai have been a people of many cattle for generations. I am not sure how many cattle I have; it is probably around six hundred. Because of the large population growth in Kenya we are being squeezed. Even many of the older ones of us see we will need to change to a new method of keeping cattle." When land is no longer abundant, the options are to fight over resources or to improve productivity on smaller herds and farms.

Through these various agricultural and educational projects, contacts between the Luo and the Maasai have increased. Although the church at Ogwedhi has not integrated (there is one Luo congregation, along with scattered groups of Maasai Christians), the Luo and Maasai attend special celebrations such as Christmas and Easter together. The project center has become a haven of sorts. When tribal leaders come to the church to settle a dispute, they leave their weapons outside the door. Cattle raids are no longer sanctioned by the tribal elders.

In 1990 a third tribe, the Kuria, agreed to work together with the Luo and Maasai in addressing long-standing community problems such as cattle raiding. Carl Hansen, a Mennonite missionary, observes, "Cattle are still being stolen as they have for centuries between the Kuria, Luo and Maasai. But a new wind is blowing that is bringing hope. If the ancient enemies can now sit and plan together, and if the new Christians can join together and help each other, there is hope that a cure for this centuries-old 'disease' is close at hand."

Ogwada, whose vision for this project was so instrumental, concludes, "The hope for our future in Kenya lies in getting our people to work together to become productive farmers. The Ogwedhi-Sigawa project has been and will be a great asset in helping that to happen."[1]

Christ or Country?

During World War I, conscientious objection to military service was not tolerated in the United States. Conscientious objectors (COs) often obeyed their draft orders and went to military training camps, where their convictions against military involvement obliged them to refuse all military duty. They were frequently mistreated in response. David, Michael and Joseph Hofer and Jacob Wipf were four young men who chose to risk severe treatment rather than compromise their belief in Christ's way of peace.

All four of these men were Hutterites, members of a communal tradition that grew out of the Anabaptist movement in Reformation Europe. During the intense persecution of the times, that occurred in the early years of the movement, the Hutterites (named for their founder Jakob Hutter) pooled their resources so that none would go hungry. They continue to live communally today.

As the four Hutterites traveled from their home in South Dakota to the military camp in Lewis, Washington, their troubles began right away. The other young men on the train tried to cut the Hutterites' hair and beards, treating them roughly and with contempt.

When they arrived at camp, they were asked to sign a card promising obedience to all military commands. As absolute objectors to all military service on the basis of their religious convictions, they refused any service within the military. They were commanded to line up with the others and march to the exercise grounds. They refused, and would not accept the uniform either. They were immediately put in the guard house.

After two months in the guard house they were court-martialed and sentenced to thirty-seven years, with a reduced sentence of twenty years, in the military prison on the island of Alcatraz.

Chained together two by two, hands and feet, they traveled under armed guard. By day the fetters on their ankles were unlocked, but never the handcuffs. At night they had to lie two by two, flat on their backs, doubly chained together. They slept little during the two nights of the journey.

When they arrived at Alcatraz, their clothes were taken from them and they were ordered to put on the military uniform, which they again refused to do. They were then put into solitary confinement in dark, dirty, stinking cells. The uniforms were thrown down next to them with the warning, "If you don't give in, you'll stay here till you die, like the four we dragged out of here yesterday." So they were locked up wearing nothing but their light underwear.

The first four-and-a-half days they got nothing to eat, and only half a glass of water each day. At night they slept on the wet and cold concrete floor without blankets. Their cell was below sea level, and water oozed through the walls.

For the last day-and-a-half they stood with their hands tied together crosswise above their heads and fastened to iron rods so high they could barely touch the floor with their feet. This strained the tendons in their arms so badly that David Hofer said after his release that he could still feel the effects in his sides. He tried to ease the terrible pain by pushing the toilet bucket toward himself with one foot and then standing on it. The four could not speak to each other because they were too far apart, but once David heard Jacob Wipf cry out: "O Almighty God!"

At the end of five days they were brought out of the dungeon into the yard, where a group of other prisoners stood. One of the other prisoners said with tears in his eyes: "Isn't it a shame to treat people like that?" The men were covered with a rash, badly bitten by insects, and their arms so swollen that they could not get their jackets on. They had been beaten with clubs. Michael Hofer was once beaten so severely that he passed out.

They continued to go without food for the fifth day until supper. After that they were locked up again in their cells day and night. On Sundays they were allowed to walk for an hour in the fenced-in courtyard, but under heavy guard. They spent four months in the prison of Alcatraz this way.

In late November, guarded by six armed sergeants and chained together two by two, they were transferred from Alcatraz to Fort Leavenworth in Kansas. After four days and five nights of travel, they arrived at eleven o'clock one night in Leavenworth, and were loudly driven up the street to the military prison with bayonets, like pigs. Chained together at the wrists, they carried their bags in their free hand and their Bibles and an extra pair of shoes under their arms. By the time they reached the prison gate they were sweating so much that their hair was wet. In this condition, in the raw winter air, they had to take off their clothes in order to put on the prison garb that was to be brought to them. When the clothes finally came two hours later, they were chilled to the bone. Early in the morning, at five o'clock, they again had to stand outside a door in the cold wind and wait. Joseph and Michael Hofer could bear it no longer— they had to be taken to the hospital.

Jacob Wipf and David Hofer were put in solitary confinement because they again refused to take up prison work under military control. Their hands were stretched out through the iron bars and chained together. They stood that way for nine hours a day, getting only bread and water. This lasted two weeks; then they received regular meals for two weeks, and so on alternately.

When the two Hofer brothers became critically ill, Jacob Wipf sent a telegram home to their wives, who left their children and traveled to Kansas the same night, accompanied by a relative. Confusion at the railroad station caused a day's delay, and when they finally reached Fort Leavenworth at eleven o'clock at night, they found their husbands close to death and hardly able to speak.

The next morning, when they were allowed to come in again, Joseph Hofer was already dead and his body in a coffin. They were told he could not be seen anymore. But his wife Maria made her way to the commanding officer in spite of guards and doors and pleaded to see her husband once more. They showed her where the body was. She went and looked through tears into the coffin, but to her horror she saw that her beloved husband had been put into the military uniform he had so valiantly refused to wear while living.

His brother Michael, who died a few days later, was dressed in his own clothes, according to the strongly expressed wish of his father, who had arrived in the meantime. When Michael died, his father, his wife and his brother David were present.

After the relatives had left with the body, David Hofer was returned to his cell and chained. Later he reported, "The whole next day I stood there and wept. I could not even wipe away my tears because my hands were chained to the prison bars." The next morning one of the guards took a message from David to the commanding officer. He asked to have a cell closer to Jacob Wipf, so that they could at least see each other, even if they would not be allowed to speak together. An hour later the guard returned and told David to pack up his things—he had been released!

On December 6, 1918, the Secretary of War issued an order prohibiting the punishment of military prisoners by handcuffing and chaining. But five days later, when two Hutterite brothers visited Jacob Wipf in Fort Leavenworth, they found him still in solitary confinement, his hands chained to the iron bars for nine hours a day, with short breaks for meals. At six each afternoon his chains were taken off. He was given four blankets for the night but had to sleep on the concrete floor.

Jacob Wipf sent the following message home with the visitors: "Sometimes I envy the three who have already been released from this torment. Then I think, why is the hand of the Lord so heavy upon me? I have always tried to be faithful and hardworking and have hardly ever made any trouble for the Brotherhood. Why must I go on suffering all alone? But then there is joy too, when I think that the Lord considers me worthy to suffer for his sake. And I must confess that my life here, compared with our previous experiences at Alcatraz, is like living in a palace."

On December 12, 1918, the chaining of military prisoners was finally discontinued in accordance with the order of the Secretary of War. The solitary prisoners received planks on the floor to sleep on, making it considerably warmer than the bare concrete floor. There were more improvements after Christmas, when the Department of War received many petitions on behalf of the prisoners.

Jacob Wipf was finally released on April 13, 1919.[1]

Working for the National Police

Elena Munoz* is a Latin American Christian who joined the Mennonite church in her country. At the time, she was employed by the National Police Training Center. As she learned more about the links between the police and the military in her country, she became uneasy about her employment. She wondered if her employment could be reconciled with her new understanding of Christ's call to peace.

W hen Elena began her job as secretary to the director of the National Police Training Center, her work included secretarial duties and the teaching of basic writing skills to the new police recruits.

"It was a good job," remembers Elena. "I had stability and good connections to people of power and influence. I could get things done.

"Before I took the job, I always thought of the police as the typical traffic cops on the corner. They directed traffic, and were generally helpful to people."

Soon after her employment began, Elena discovered that the police had very close connections to the military. "There was a secret U.S. military base beside the Police Training Center, and people frequently went back and forth. The purpose of this base was to provide training to the Special Forces of the military who were also close by.

"The higher echelon of police all had military backgrounds. It was not possible to become a high ranking police officer without military experience.

During my seven years there, my bosses included an Army major,

* Fictitious name

a police colonel and an Army colonel who later became the head of military intelligence."

Elena was not prepared for this close connection between the police and the military. In fact, her lack of familiarity with "military culture" sometimes created problems: "I did not know military rank and protocol very well, so I did not always use the proper names when addressing my superiors. As a civilian, I did not feel that I should have to pay attention to all of the proper military titles. On several occasions, I was charged with insubordination."

Elena's many opportunities for interaction with the recruits gave her a window on their lives and their difficulties. "The physical training was very harsh. The recruits suffered from both physical abuse and from neglect by structures that didn't respond to their needs. Many of the recruits were afraid to take their problems to their superiors. I felt sorry for them, and often referred specific cases to the director for investigation.

"Three years after I began my job, in 1985, I joined the Mennonite church. I knew about the Mennonite teaching against military service, but at that time, I wanted to continue my job. I wanted to be the presence of Christ among the recruits. Somebody needed to show compassion toward them. They too were God's people.

"In my country, police recruits are not forced into service. Instead, potential police recruits are told about the many opportunities for education or for promotion to positions of responsibility, as an incentive for enlistment. Many of these promises never come true.

"As I learned to know the recruits, I discovered that it was difficult social conditions like poverty and unemployment that put them there. Ninety percent of the people in the military and police came from rural and peasant backgrounds."

Elena became more and more uncomfortable with her working environment, and began looking for other opportunities. To her surprise, she learned that she was being considered for the International Visitor Exchange Program of Mennonite Central Committee, which gave her the opportunity to work in the United States for one year. She was accepted into the program, and negotiated a one-year leave of absence from her job. She wanted to keep her job because she was supporting her sister's secondary education.

While in the U.S. she had an opportunity to see her country from another point of view. "Someone from my country was brought to the United States for trial by the U.S. Drug Enforcement Agency.

This was done without due process, a violation of my government's constitution. Since I had worked for a part of the government which agreed to this injustice, I felt betrayed.

"During my time in the U.S. I also learned of a connection between the national police and an Army battalion which was linked to death squads. So when I returned to my country, I decided that it was time to change jobs.

"As a follower of Christ, who came to bring news of peace and to reconcile peoples, I am called to take peace to others. I cannot take the life of my neighbor, for my neighbor is created in the image of God. God has called us through Christ to preserve life. Armies are synonymous with death.

"The budgets of many Latin American countries are to a large degree absorbed by the military, while the funds for health, education and housing are cut back. We should advocate for justice so that there will be peace."

Elena tried to resign from her position at the Police Training Center when she returned to her country. She was told that this would not be possible, because she had been given a leave of absence and the job had been held open for her. She was offered better positions, including training in computers and language courses. She declined these offers and was eventually allowed to leave.

Elena now serves as the secretary for the Mennonite Peace and Justice Committee in her country. The Peace and Justice Committee is working with four different denominations toward the goal of establishing alternate service provisions for conscientious objectors. Youth education is another aspect of the committee's work. "In young people is the future of a people," notes Elena. "The youth can do much for their country. We should take advantage of their energy, intelligence and gifts to do positive things."

Inviting the IRS to Dinner

Paul Leatherman, of Lancaster, Pennsylvania, has withheld his war taxes for twenty years. During that time, he and his wife Loretta (now deceased) have endured tax audits, court hearings and seized bank accounts. Paul has taken the time to visit with Internal Revenue Service agents at his home and place of work. Through articles and interviews in church periodicals, Paul has explained their convictions about not paying taxes for war to his community of faith.

In explaining their motivation for war tax resistance, Paul and Loretta referred to the scriptures and to their experiences in Vietnam, where they worked with Mennonite Central Committee.

W e saw the war effort change from manpower to money power," explained Loretta. "Men aren't used as much anymore and, instead, our money was being used to do intensive bombing. We would not go to war ourselves and so we thought we should resist having our money being sent to war also."

Paul continues, "I think serving in Vietnam radicalized us in that sense. About every night we were there, we went to sleep with the sound of bombing, and from our house we saw bombs exploding. We lived in the middle of the war and saw what it did to children and families. We saw our tax dollars dismember and disembowel those whom we knew as friends in Christ."

"We ought to render unto Caesar or anybody else what is their due. We also give unto God what is due—that is the important thing. Our duty to obey government and to pay taxes is in a context that includes feeding our enemy and never taking revenge. When God and Caesar come into conflict, then my moral, ethical training is to not pay Caesar."

Initially, the Leathermans withheld the percentage of their taxes equal to the military portion of federal spending (50-60%). This led them into the courts, and into direct contact with IRS agents charged with the responsibility of collecting the owed taxes.

"One of the first years we resisted paying war taxes," notes Paul, "we owed a little bit of money at the end of the year. We claimed a war tax credit and asked for a refund. The IRS turned it down and called us in to audit the credit and also our contributions, which were somewhat above the norm. The inspector took twenty-five minutes to audit our contributions and concluded that they were exactly right to the penny. He said that was fine, but that he simply could not allow the war tax credit, and it was no use talking about it."

"'Now look,' I said, 'you asked us to come in here for an audit and we had to leave our jobs to come. You've taken twenty-five minutes of my time auditing something which I knew all along was correct and I'm equally convinced that I'm entitled to the war tax credit. I'd like at least twenty-five minutes of your time to discuss it.'

"He said, 'Okay, let's talk.' We discussed the pros and cons of why we were opposed to paying war taxes. He listened and sort of entered into the discussion and then at the end of twenty-five minutes, I said, 'Well, you've given me twenty-five minutes, but there are still many things we could talk about. Would you be interested in reading a little more about this?'

"He said he would, so I gave him Kaufman's *What Belongs to Caesar?*[1] and a few other things. Then I said, 'After you've had a chance to read these, why don't you come over for dinner next Wednesday and we can talk about it some more?'

"He accepted the invitation. We weren't sure if he would come, but he showed up and we had a very good discussion with him for about three hours. He was very much against the Vietnam War but he thought that our tax resistance was completely useless and that there was no way to succeed.

"On another occasion, an IRS agent came to see me at the Mennonite Central Committee office, where I was working. The receptionist called me and told me there was someone out there to see me, but I didn't recognize his name. Only when I got out there and he showed me his credentials did I realize who he was. That was when we had the open office at MCC, so rather than taking him into a conference room, I brought him in beside my desk. I wanted to be on my own turf when he questioned me.

"He asked me about our tax bill and I said, "Yes, I acknowledge that from the IRS perspective and the judge's perspective, it is a legitimate bill, but I don't have any intention of paying it.' He replied that he was here to collect the bill and he didn't expect to leave until

I paid it.

"'Well,' I said, 'I already told you that I don't expect to pay it and since I'm not going to pay it, I think you ought to put me in jail. My wife has been expecting that you might come around sometime and she said that if I go to jail, she'd like to know where I'm going so she could write to me. I would also like to know how soon it would be so that I can make arrangements for somebody to take my place at this desk.' He looked at me and said he had never heard anybody talk like that before. He went up to the bank the next day and issued an order to draw the money out of my bank account.

"I must admit that even when I was talking to him I didn't think I was risking a jail sentence. I didn't think the IRS would put anyone in jail, because they have other ways to collect the money."

In 1981, after ten years of fairly intensive tax resistance and scrutiny by the IRS, Paul adopted a new way of expressing his convictions about military taxes. Rather than withholding a percentage equal to the military portion of federal spending, Paul decided to withhold $7.77, a symbolic amount.

"Despite our best efforts, the IRS always got its money. While our tax resistance had afforded unique opportunities for witness, we began to feel tired. Tax resistance takes a lot of energy and time.

"We began to wonder what next step a larger group of Mennonites might take. A symbolic $7.77 war tax deduction helped us be counted as conscientious objectors. Yet it was no more radical or illegal than asking our youth to register as conscientious objectors when there was no legal provision to do so.

"Why $7.77? Seven is the perfect number in the Bible. Jesus tells us to forgive seventy times seven. While any amount might do, $7.77 had special meaning to us. Seven dollars and seventy-seven cents becomes a frustration to the IRS. It is too small and too costly to collect. Much discussion can follow."

To Paul's knowledge, his dream of ten thousand people symbolically withholding $7.77 from their federal tax payments each year has not materialized. Yet he continues the practice. "It would be highly significant if ten thousand people did this," says Paul. "Symbolic withholding allows you to make your case with some visibility, without all the negative consequences that come from withholding larger amounts. I know it is timid, but each time I get a bill, I can write to my Senators, Representatives, and the President reminding them that for reasons of conscience, I cannot pay. I also point to the potential for a legal alternative in the U.S. Peace Tax

Fund Bill which is introduced into Congress every year.

"Symbolic withholding allows me to at least do something in support of conscientious objection to war. I'm not a purist, or I would have been in jail all this time. I support those who act more courageously and withhold larger amounts as long as they can handle it financially. I also support those who limit their incomes to decrease their tax liability. There are many ways to do this, but none of us can save the world. We can witness to the world, but it is the Lord who will bring in the Kingdom."[2]

I Have No Enemies

In the year 1572, Jan Smit, a Mennonite from Northern Holland was captured and put into prison because of his Anabaptist beliefs. The era was one of intense conflict between Spanish Catholic rule and local Dutch nobles who were sympathetic to the Protestant cause. The town in which Jan was imprisoned was overtaken by the Protestants, and Jan was released. A short time later, he was captured by a Spanish navy captain.

During this second imprisonment, Jan's captors decided that he should join other prisoners as oarsmen on Haarlem Lake for a battle against Protestant-held Haarlem. When Jan was brought to the boat, however, he declared that he had no enemies, and could not in good conscience row the boat.

His captors questioned him on matters of faith, and threatened him. They could not move Jan to renounce his faith and return to the boat as an oarsman, so they sentenced him to be hung from the gallows by one leg until dead.[1]

We Are Still Friends

In 1986, Rob and Sandi Thompson attended the Christmas Eve service at Mt. Pleasant Mennonite Church, in Chesapeake, Virginia. "We were mildly surprised by the invitation," remembers Robert, "but as career Navy people who were always moving around, we were not shy. We decided to go."

That Christmas Eve service began a warm and respectful relationship between the Thompsons and Mt. Pleasant Church. After attending Mt. Pleasant for some time, however, it became apparent to the Thompsons that differences in culture and belief systems would make church membership difficult. At the heart of the matter was the question of peace and military service. Was this a matter of salvation, or simply a cultural tradition?

"I grew up with a strong sense of patriotism," recalls Rob, whose father served in World War II. "As a family, we frequently went to Veterans of Foreign Wars activities. I participated in Boy Scouts and school activities which helped me learn to love and respect my country."

Rob joined the Army at the beginning of his senior year of high school and served for three years. When he graduated from college in 1975, Rob found that a career in the Navy offered a better salary and more opportunities than the other options open to him. He has been on active duty ever since.

"We felt warmly welcomed and accepted as people at Mt. Pleasant," recalls Sandi. "At that time very few people knew that we were a part of the military." And it seemed to make little difference to church members as people learned of their employment.

"We taught Sunday School, Bible School, and led a Bible study on Wednesday evening. We grew closer to many in the congregation. Some of the older ones seemed to keep their distance, but we understood that. We tried not to bring our Navy connection into our conversations at the church. Rob never wore his uniform."

"The Thompsons were very committed to Christ," recalls Robert

---

Mast, pastor at Mt. Pleasant. "We appreciated their testimony and spirit very much. They were frequent participants in our sharing time during Sunday morning services. Their children were active participants in the Sunday School and other church programs."

In this context the Thompsons expressed interest in church membership. This stirred some discussion within the congregation, and the Thompsons became aware of the strong concerns some members had about their employment with the Navy. "The expressions of concern about our membership were informal," note the Thompsons. "It seemed that the leaders and most of the members supported our request. But we could see that several families were deeply troubled."

According to Pastor Mast, concern regarding church membership for military families at Mt. Pleasant grows out of biblical understandings and congregational history. "Most members believe that destruction of enemies and participation in any war is a violation of Christ's call to be a disciple. During World War I, one of our members was imprisoned for his commitment to Christ's way of peace. At a recent winter Bible School class, we studied the biblical basis for nonresistance. This commitment to peace is something we have stressed with some consistency over the years."

Given this background, in August of 1987 church leadership requested counsel from the congregation on the issue of membership for military people. While this request for counsel was not tied directly to the Thompsons' membership request, most people knew of their interest. The report on the congregation's counsel, dated September 28, 1987, noted that the membership reaffirmed its commitment to peace and nonresistance, and to a lifestyle based on the love of Christ. Many also stated their desire to accept as members all who confess Jesus as Savior, recognizing honest differences in application.

In the fall of 1987, Pastor Mast met personally with a number of members in the congregation to hear their concerns about the issue of membership for military personnel. His report to the church council summarizes two different responses of members of the congregation:

1. We must follow the New Testament pattern of welcoming all believers in Jesus as Saviour and Lord. We have persons "limping" along in the fellowship for other reasons including drugs, divorce, affluence, etc. If we can risk having a less-than-perfect fellowship for these things, can we not also risk military membership?

---

2. But how can we preach peace with career military personnel in the congregation? What about funerals with full military honors? How about teaching peace to our children, and the influence of example?

Following this process of testing and discernment, congregational leadership decided to move ahead with plans to accept the Thompsons as members of the church. In late March, 1988, it was announced to the congregation that the Thompsons would be received into membership the following Sunday.

By this time the Thompsons were having serious second thoughts about proceeding with membership. It was awkward to be the cause of dissension in the congregation. "The last thing we wanted to do was cause a split within the church," notes Rob.

Sandi felt particularly reluctant to move ahead without unanimous support from church members. "In past congregations," recalls Sandi, "whenever we received a new member, everyone stood up as a sign of welcome. In the Mennonite church, only those who support the new member stand up. I had a real problem with the thought of not being fully supported, after a year and a half of participation with the congregation."

The Thompsons temporarily withdrew their membership request. The next Sunday, the following announcement appeared in the bulletin: "Rob and Sandi Thompson have decided to postpone their membership until a time when the congregation is more ready to receive them."

What began as a temporary postponement eventually resulted in the Thompsons joining another church. Rob and the family were transferred to Spain for two years. Upon their return to the Chesapeake area, they began worshipping at a large Assemblies of God congregation, while maintaining personal friendships with members of Mt. Pleasant Mennonite Church.

"I came away from the church convinced that their beliefs in peace had cultural, rather than scriptural foundations," notes Rob. "I had previously thought that peace was a belief which Mennonites based squarely on scripture, but I didn't find that to be the case. Peace was not central to the worship experience or congregational life at Mt. Pleasant. I never heard a sermon on peace while we were there, and peace was not a central topic in scriptural discussions. The issue of peace seemed more like a secondary issue. When I asked why one family expressed concern about their daughter marrying a Sheriff's Deputy, they responded, 'Our peace belief doesn't permit that.'

"The Mennonites were handy with dogs, traps, and rifles which they used to destroy animal life," he remembers. "This seemed inconsistent to me."

On a deeper level, Rob raised the issue of economic dependence. "All the Mennonites I knew were extremely willing, and even went out of their way to do business with military people. No one declined to take money from the military. If peace and the prohibition of military service were true convictions based on scripture, then doing business with the military didn't make sense. It seemed like the members of the church who were born Mennonite simply accepted the prohibition of military service as 'part of the package,' but were not willing to be confronted by the peace issue in other areas."

Pastor Mast spoke of this inconsistency when he reflected on the dilemma presented by the militarized economy. "There is a sense in which the military has conscripted all of us," he said simply. "Tidewater area's whole construction industry would be dead if it weren't for the military. One of the members who expressed concern about the Thompsons becoming members has worked most of his life for a private contractor, whose work includes repairing Navy ships."

It was some of these perceived inconsistencies which sent Rob to the scriptures, searching to see if he had missed something. Rob also read several books on peace given to him by the leadership team at Mt. Pleasant.

"If anything," notes Rob, "my beliefs regarding the biblical basis for military service are stronger than ever. The scriptures are filled with references to military people. Nowhere does this issue seem to affect salvation. Mennonites need to understand their faith well, and answer the question, 'Can you be a Christian and not be accepted within the church?'"

Rob contrasts the emphasis on footwashing with the peace issue. "The practice of footwashing at Mt. Pleasant Church was wonderful. It has affected my life to this day. I heard sermons on footwashing, and it seemed to be a stronger issue than peace. Footwashing was biblically based and clearly taught without apology. I could relate to that."

In retrospect, the Thompsons do not feel bitter about their experience with Mt. Pleasant. They do, however, feel disappointed that the issue of church membership caused their paths to separate. "We were surprised at the emphasis on church membership," notes

Sandi. "It was alright for us to become a part of the fellowship and fully use our gifts, but the point of covenant seemed like a real big issue. I don't understand the difference."

With respect to the congregational process with the Thompsons, Pastor Mast believes the congregation acted carefully and responsibly. "I don't feel badly about the Thompsons not following through with their request," he says, "but I do regret that they are no longer worshipping with us. The congregation was very honest. No one was malicious, and our relationships were not broken. We are still friends."

Slacker, Buy Liberty Bonds

Joseph Boll of Lancaster, Pennsylvania, tells how his family was mistreated because they did not buy war bonds during World War II.

My father, a Pennsylvania farmer, was heavily pressured to buy War Bonds during World War II. He had deep convictions against supporting the war, and because of this, he suffered some rather unpleasant experiences. One day he went to the mill, and on his way home he stopped to chat with one of the neighbors who lived in a short lane. As he left to go home, several lawyers from Lancaster met him at the end of the lane. Because he would not compromise his convictions, one man pulled off his coat and said, "You are not worth any more than to be killed, and I feel like doing it right here."

I remember hearing my father relate this experience, saying how he breathed a prayer that if he was struck on the one cheek he would have grace to turn the other.

My brother Noah told me that one Saturday evening just before dark, he and some of the rest of the children were playing in the yard when some cars stopped along the road. People got out of the cars and came walking toward the children. He said he remembers that they were somewhat frightened and moved toward the house as the men started talking with them. Previous to this experience, Noah had been sent home from school because he would not salute the flag. So the men got after him about that, which of course frightened him. But my father was the one they wanted, so they proceeded to the kitchen door.

My mother went to the door with the baby in her arms and talked with them. By this time it was a large group. My mother was not sure where my father was at the time. He would either be in the barn, or at the other end of our double house with Grandpa. My Uncle John Boll and his wife were there to visit my grandfather that evening, and my father had gone over to visit with them. He did not go out of the house.

The men intended to tar and feather my father, take him to Manheim, and parade him around on the square. But instead they decorated the buildings with flags, and painted on the sandstone walks in the yard and on the buildings, "Slacker, Buy Liberty Bonds." They pushed the car out of the garage and left the air out of all the tires. They caused quite a disturbance and stayed until almost midnight. The following day there were a lot of sightseers—in the afternoon there was a continuous line of cars. Sometime later the church got together and cleaned up our farm.

As I think of this experience, what has left the deepest impression on me is the memory of my mother standing at the door with the baby in her arms and me, a trembling little boy, standing close by. As I think of this, I can't help but feel that mother standing there holding the baby was the divine providence of God. One of these hard-hearted men started opening the screen door, and another one said, "Let her alone, you also have a wife at home with a baby in her arms." I believe the Lord used this to touch their hearts, so that they did not take my father by force.[1]

On the Brink of Calamity

As Zaire struggled for independence from Belgium in the 1950s, ethnic rivalries resurfaced in a fresh way. One of the tension spots was Charlesville in the region of South Kasai, a Mennonite church center where Baluba and Lulua ethnic societies lived in close proximity. The church had worked hard to promote harmony between these two groups. Yet, as violence in the surrounding countryside escalated and relatives were being killed, Christians found it increasingly difficult to maintain their unity. Finally, in late May, 1960, the war came to Charlesville.

Baluba and Lulua young men picked up arms and began to prepare for war. Most of the Christians were also caught in the confrontation. The people of Charlesville stood at the precipice of an inevitable battle, as the two groups of warriors advanced toward each other through the center of the town.[1]

In the midst of this crisis, Pastor Kuamba, a young Lulua leader with a reputation for skilled mediation between the tribes, hurriedly called together several of the Mennonite missionaries.

Kuamba brought unusual experience to this task. For eight years he had cared for his invalid wife. She had never borne him a child. She had brought him little remuneration from her work in their fields, as wives were expected to do. For the last three years of her life she was bedfast. In spite of pressure from tribemates to abandon her, in spite of personal ridicule and public gossip, he served her in the deepest Christian meaning of the word, to her death.

Now Kuamba exhibited the wages of that service. From some deep inner resource, Kuamba drew patience and strength. He greeted the missionaries with a controlled and quiet voice.

"Matters have become very difficult now," he said. "Do you hear that noise up there on the hill? Warriors of the two sides are standing in lines facing each other. They are shouting insults at each other. They are trying to ignite the fire of war. The time has arrived for us to show our courage. Let's go walk between the lines to restrain them. We want to speak words that will cool their anger. We need to bring their minds back into paths of reason, so that they will sit down and talk."

The group prayed together, committing themselves into the hands of God. Kuamba and the three missionaries left the house and started up the hill into the residential area of the town, empty-handed, except for Kuamba, who carried his Bible. When they reached the angry, shouting mass, they passed the Baluba warriors and walked out between the lines. Both sides responded instantly.

"What are you preachers doing here? Step to one side and get out of our way. Stop getting yourselves mixed up in our affairs. We're having it out today."

The four mediators began calmly to talk with each side, trying to divert attention away from the efforts of each side to inflame the other.

One of the missionaries, Harold Graber, explained, "We are not trying to interfere in your affairs. Our desire is to save your lives and property. Put down your weapons. The moment a drop of human blood is shed, what will happen? People created by a God of love do not resolve their problems by butchering each other. They solve their problems by using their minds. If people out in the hill villages want to fight, that is their business. But we are people of God. This is the ground of the mission station. It belongs to God. It is hallowed ground. Human blood will not be shed here. Not a single drop."

Alone among the local church leaders to risk exposing himself, Pastor Kuamba stood in an open yard between two homes in the center of the conflict area. He raised his voice in entreaty: "My friends, my kinsmen. Why are you rushing so rapidly in the direction of fighting? Take your thinking out of the path of war. Don't you fear the warnings of our ancestors about shedding human blood? Fighting will destroy everything. It will divide us perpetually. We are Christians. There is another way to resolve our differences."

After some hesitation and more encouragement from the tiny group of mediators, the chiefs of each side decided to each bring three of their warriors together for a peace parley.

Some warriors protested vehemently. Others reluctantly agreed and proceeded to select their representatives. Slowly, conferees responded. They gave their weapons to others, cautiously approached each other on the neutral ground between the lines, and began to consult.

A few combatants, still determined to fight, persisted in shouting insults. Chiefs ordered them to keep quiet and to hold their positions.

Negotiations continued for about an hour. Tension between the participants subsided to the point where the church leaders and chiefs won the support of the warrior delegations to abandon plans for confrontation and to work for reconciliation. They prayed together, and the tribal groups returned to their respective lines to announce their decisions.

"We are your chiefs. It is our responsibility to govern you. We want you to leave this dispute in our hands. We will take care of it. That person who rejects our authority and starts pursuing a different path will bear his burden. Go to your homes quietly."

After some initial protest, the warriors slowly obeyed. Grumbling, they began to disperse. They sat at their homes that afternoon. A few of them continued to shout angry challenges at each other from their respective yards, but by evening all was quiet.[2]

I Would Like to Keep My Beliefs

Rudy Yoder, an Amish man from Millersburg, Ohio, was twenty-three years old in 1918 when he received his draft notice.

Rudy traveled by train from Ohio to Camp Jefferson, located near Jefferson City, Missouri. "I felt so terribly alone," noted Rudy as he recalled the day of his military registration. "I felt the kind of weakness a person feels when he faces an overwhelming uncertainty."

When Rudy met the registration officer, he said, "Mister, I am sorry, but I cannot fight. I am a conscientious objector. I don't believe it is right to go to war. I would like to keep my beliefs."

To Rudy's surprise, the officer did not confront or threaten him for his stand. Instead, he told Rudy that the matter could be taken care of later, and showed Rudy to his tent.

The next morning Rudy found a uniform laid out on his bed. He was told to appear for inspection in fifteen minutes' time. His initial impulse was to not wear the uniform, but after some thought he decided to put it on. "Battling against my conscience, I was swept along in the current. After breakfast the captain announced that the first training would be to learn how to march.

"One day followed another. All of them were packed with activity. I still wore the uniform and marched and followed commands as war skills were drilled into the draftees.

"I studied my New Testament daily, realizing more and more what I should do. I wished I had never put on the uniform or started taking training. It seemed so much harder to quit now, than if I had never begun.

"I knew that rifle training would come up next, and I decided that would be my stopping place. My will was at battle with my conscience. My entire home training urged me to refuse to be a part of this legalized training for war. Yet here I was the only one who had these convictions. I was the only one who might have to give his life for his faith.

"'Left, right. Left, right. Halt. Shoulder your guns. Fire!' How different these curt, crisp commands were from the earnest pleas of Jesus, 'Love your enemies. Resist not evil. If my kingdom were of this world then would my servants fight. Walk in love as Christ has also loved us.'

After two weeks, Rudy decided not to wear his uniform. One morning he placed his uniform into his laundry bag, and walked into the mess hall dressed in his plain Amish clothes. To his surprise, no one reacted. Several days later, however, two officers confronted him.

"Yoder, you come with us and don't try any tricks. You should wear a uniform," snapped one officer as they guided Rudy past the barracks and up a steep hill.

"I don't believe that war is right, because the New Testament teaches us not to kill," replied Rudy. To his surprise he felt no fear.

The officers showed Rudy three fresh graves in the hillside. "That's what's going to happen to you if you don't wear your uniform," the officers told Rudy. "Those boys refused to wear them, and look where they are now. Take your choice. If you don't comply with our rules, you will be the fourth."

As Rudy considered his answer, one of the officers continued, "We'll give you until tomorrow morning. If you don't give up by then, you'll fill the fourth grave."

Slowly Rudy responded. "You don't have to wait until tomorrow morning. I have made my decision. I am ready now."

To their repeated threats, Rudy replied, "I won't change my decision. You need not wait." Seeing their efforts were in vain, the officers returned Rudy to his barracks.

While he continued to be the object of some harrassment, Rudy was never threatened in this way again. Later he was transferred to Camp Sherman, where nearly one hundred conscientious objectors were held. On January 6, 1919, just thirteen weeks after his induction, Rudy was released, and returned home.[1]

No Taxes for Vengeance

One group of Anabaptists which formed in Eastern Europe came to be known as the Hutterian Brethren. Hutterites are distinctive from other Anabaptist groups in that they hold all goods in a common purse. They trace their origins to 1528, when a group of about two hundred persons were forced to leave the town of Nikolsburg, Moravia because they refused to accept the dominant Reformation view that Christians could retain the use of the sword. Known as "staff-bearers" (as opposed to "sword-bearers"), they were finally ordered by Lord Leonhard von Liechtenstein to leave his land. With few resources at hand, the people pooled their goods so that all would be supported.

From their beginnings in the sixteenth century, the Hutterites believed that not only must Christians reject the use of the sword, but they must also refuse to pay war taxes. The first real test of this principle came in 1579, when Moravia imposed a new tax to be paid by all citizens over sixteen years of age. Their response is related in The Chronicle of the Hutterian Brethren.

W e could not pay the tax because it was for war purposes, and that is not in accord with our faith in Christ, who demands a peaceful people. So we became the object of hostility from the lords in Moravia, who sent their servants to count the people in our houses, and took the tax accordingly in livestock. Some took it from what they owed us for our work. We could only lay it all before the Lord our God and choose to suffer robbery than willingly give anything and defile our consciences.

After a decade, the authorities themselves grew tired of the confiscations and of our protesting and complaining. Several lords asked us again that we tell them what we could do that was not against our conscience. They said we should realize that since we enjoyed the benefits of the country and could practice our trades, they could not exempt us completely. If a large group such as ours were to pay nothing at all, that would place the burden on the Provincial Diet.

So the elders and brothers from all our communities met to decide whether we could give something for the good of the country that did not go against our conscience.

The following letter was then sent to Lord Friedrich von Zerotin to present to the Provincial Diet:

We wish His Lordship now and always everything good from the almighty God! His Lordship realizes our difficulties in regard to paying taxes, and other lords on whose land we live are troubled (like His Lordship himself) at having to take our horses, oxen, and other things instead, as has been happening for some time. They see this as lamentable, which it certainly is, and have requested us to find some other way to help the country that is not against our conscience. We considered this seriously, for we do not want to be a burden, but for the good of the country we will gladly do something that is not against our conscience.

Our greatest fear, however (and we beg His Lordship not to take it amiss), is that only the name but not the tax would be changed, so that we would be led into it before we could turn around. If we then discovered that it was used for war or for other purposes we oppose, this would distress us greatly. If it should come to this, we would prefer to have our goods and chattels taken as hitherto rather than in any way support deeds of vengeance and so stain our conscience. We say this in the fear of God, for we pay no taxes for vengeance, nor do we give anything as substitute for such taxes.

We can only give what would benefit the country in some other way, as we realize that we enjoy the benefits of the country and are allowed to buy the grain we need wherever it is available. In order not to encumber the country, we would like to support ourselves by our own trades and live off the land.

We would be willing to pay an annual sum on each house where we have a communal kitchen, as long as we can be assured that the money will be used profitably for the country and for people in need. God knows that we would do whatever we can to avoid being a burden to anyone. Yet we would ask that the sum not be higher than we can afford to pay and that it not be increased, because we have among us many sick, weak, and disabled people to care for.

We must expect times of distress, not knowing what God may allow to come upon us as a test of our faith. As we may have to move out of our houses or be driven from them into destitution, we cannot bind ourselves to make these payments. But since we are so often reproached with enjoying the benefits of the country without being willing to do anything for it, we thought it necessary to write our answer to His Lordship in all good faith. We are not opposed to doing our part if it can be done in God's name and without damage to our conscience. We wish to offer our help in whatever serves a good cause, to the best of our ability and as long as God grants it.

It is our humble request that His Lordship will not be displeased at our simple statement but will present our case to the Diet on our behalf. Plead with them on our behalf to have patience with us, for we have been driven into this land as strangers for the sake of our faith. We want to be patient, remaining hopeful and praying without ceasing that God will grant peace to our governing authorities and to Moravia, so that we, in their peace, may also experience peace. May God grant it. With this we wish His Lordship happiness and well-being.

> Dated Neumühl, May 14, 1590
> From the elders of the Church
> that men call Hutterian

This arrangement brought relief for a time. However, in 1596, the lords again confiscated goods in lieu of war taxes. And each year for the next twenty-five years, they again confiscated livestock, wine, grain and other things from some of our communities because, as in the beginning, we had refused for conscience' sake to pay the very heavy war taxes. Finally, in 1622, after suffering much from repeated wars and plundering armies, an especially heavy war tax was imposed. When we protested, the ruling Cardinal told the Emperor that the Hutterites were rebels, enemies of His Majesty and had caused him nothing but trouble during the war. The Cardinal was then given authority to evict us from Moravia, which he proceeded to do.[1]

Why Not Take Risks for Something With Real Meaning?

Harold and Rita* recently joined another family in purchasing unworked land in South Dakota. The two families will work the land to bring it into production. A long-term dream of Harold and Rita's, the move is rooted in care and concern for the environment, a belief in simplicity and a commitment to Christ's way of peace.

Military tax-resistance is one aspect of these concerns to which Harold and Rita are committed. On a practical level, however, it has been a difficult and ever-changing struggle.

"We first talked in depth about tax resistance during our work in Africa with Mennonite Central Committee. Several events, such as the bombing of Libya and the invasion of Grenada, forced us to think more about the U.S. role in the world and how its military actions were financed. In our overseas setting, we felt more personally connected to such events.

"We've never had doubts from a scriptural standpoint that tax resistance is right. Since our time in Africa that has been clear to us. In fact, when we latched onto the idea it was a real relief to finally find a response to violence that made sense. It seemed clear that if we oppose violence with our words, then we shouldn't pay for it. It is a simple idea, but in practical terms, it becomes very complex."

"I think the reason I didn't see the sense of tax resistance earlier is that I didn't see examples or models of active peacemaking before," explains Rita. "I had heard a lot of talk about it, which is important, but I didn't see the models. I also heard the admonitions to 'give to

* Names and locations are fictitious

Caesar what is Caesar's.' We didn't ask a lot of questions in my home community, because the economy was dominated by military-related jobs. But the seeds of peace theology were sown, and sprouted into real life later."

When Harold and Rita returned to the States, the church community in which they settled was not one which nurtured their budding commitment to tax resistance. "We knew we couldn't be tax resisters in isolation," continues Rita. "So we looked for ways to find support. After about a year, we moved to New York where we had friends who were already doing tax resistance.

"We formed a type of community with our friends. We lived in the same house. We shared rent and utilities, which kept our living expenses very low, but we kept our finances separate.

"During those years we tried to limit our incomes so that we could take care of our own children and do other things in the community. We didn't want a lifestyle that required two incomes per family. This also allowed us to live below the taxable level. We didn't have to pay any federal income taxes, and thereby avoided paying taxes for the military. On such low incomes, there were times when we had to help each other out.

"Now we have moved to South Dakota to pursue something we have always wanted to do. We have purchased land together with another couple. We have consciously chosen to be dependent on one another. It is counter-culture in every way.

"In some ways a choice like this makes life infinitely easier, because some decisions are made for us. For example, when we moved we had few housing options, because we had no savings. We couldn't afford much. Friends of ours were troubled because they bought a house which required them to make a lot of money. It is this kind of choice which precludes tax resistance for many people, rather than genuine struggles with scripture.

"There are difficulties, however. We feel much more vulnerable in our current setting. Once again we are living on just one income. The economy in this community is very poor, and we have discovered that it is hard to stick to your ideals in a bad economy. In New York we lived in a prosperous community and had all kinds of job choices. Here we can neither choose our job nor our income. We have to take what we can get.

"Now I almost find myself resenting our former choice to limit our incomes when we had the option of earning more. We are living with the results of that choice and have no savings to fall back on. One of our big worries is health care and health insurance. We had to raise the deductible on our health insurance because we couldn't afford to pay the high premiums. We have two children with a third one on the way. We are so close to the edge at the moment that if we were offered a good job which put us over the taxable level, I think we'd take it. We would then have to deal with what that means for tax resistance.

"Tax resistance is not as central a motivation for what we are doing as it used to be. It has moved off center because our income is nowhere near the taxable level. This is a life-long issue, always changing with the stages of life, and requires constant decision-making. The cost of living does vary for people. At certain points in life you might have need for a lot of money. I feel less and less that everybody ought to do tax resistance the way we do.

"I also have a fear of failure. I can't say that we will always be committed to tax resistance. We have family members who would be happy to point out that we were wrong. In a sense, my fear of failure comes from pride.

"At times we wonder if living below the taxable level is effective as a means of tax resistance. We haven't had to explain our tax resistance to the IRS or to anybody because we haven't earned enough money now for five years to file. So sometimes we feel like, 'What's the point?' But our lifestyle makes people look twice.

"Despite the economic difficulties, I would rate our quality of life at one hundred percent. It is wonderful. We are so happy here. It feels good to help reclaim a piece of land. That's part of our commitment. I also volunteer at a local center for abused women and children. Every time I go there I realize how lucky I am. I am so thankful. In all the important ways we have really got it made.

"Tax resistance is not a closed issue. As we change and as children grow, we will go through different stages with difficult risks to take in each stage. Why not take risks for something which has real meaning?

"I always think about this in terms of how Jesus would live. Jesus would not take the easy way out or buy into the system. Everything Jesus taught and stood for would have opposed military power, and lifestyles which are built on it. I don't understand all the difficult passages about taxes, but I think of Jesus' teaching to love our neighbors as ourselves. How can you do that with weapons and with affluent lifestyles that bring injustice to millions of people?"

Deserting the Military

During the Vietnam War, military service was mandatory for all Vietnamese men, with the exception of religious leaders and certain hardship cases. Terms of service were through age forty-five, or till the end of the war. Conscientious objection was not a legal right.

P han van Khai, a member of one of the Mennonite fellowships, had joined the army as required by law. Later, however, he became uneasy with the prospect of killing other human beings. Mr. Phan's faith and his understanding of the Bible taught him that a child of God cannot kill. He decided to desert.

Deserting the army was an illegal act, and could have resulted in severe consequences for Mr. Phan. One of the Vietnamese Mennonite leaders says, "The treatment of deserters depended on the events of the war. If things were tense, the military would try to catch deserters, and would punish them severely in order to make others obey the law. If the war situation was more relaxed, the military didn't care so much about deserters.

"It was very difficult for deserters to avoid detection. The police would frequently surround a neighborhood in the evening, and check the papers of each household. I think Mr. Phan had some false papers."

Mr. Phan's decision to leave the military was not an issue of contention in the Mennonite fellowship, even though some members of the fellowship were in the military. "I didn't want this to divide the people," noted his pastor. "This issue could have divided both the fellowship and some of the families. I respected the choices which my brothers and sisters made. I tried to help with Bible teaching, and noted that Jesus taught us not to use force to resolve problems.

"Mature Christians found it easier to understand and apply Jesus' teaching. It was very difficult, however, for new Christians

---

to avoid joining the military. Each family made its own decision.

"I tried to help Mr. Phan. But I told him to be very careful, because if he were caught, we could all be in trouble. The church could have been closed because we were helping a deserter."

But Mr. Phan was very careful about avoiding military check points, and managed to go undetected throughout the rest of the war.

Impossible Choices

Anyone who has read the New Testament cannot dare to kill anyone," he* said with conviction. "In Ethiopia, this is very difficult, however. People have no choice. Young men must serve in the military and all who earn more than thirty-five dollars per month must pay taxes."

He continued sadly, "Some of my relatives and friends have been killed or have killed in the military. As a result of much poverty and injustice, our society is very violent. Young men are expected to stand up and fight for their family and the motherland. Refusing to serve in the army is considered irresponsible and unacceptable. I have heard that several Jehovah's Witnesses were shot when they refused to serve in the army or pay war taxes.

"Initially, when North American Mennonite missionaries tried to talk to us about nonresistance, I found this teaching very difficult to accept. Gradually, however, my convictions changed. I studied Jesus' teachings, I read the stories of Anabaptist martyrs in Holland and I was challenged by the witness and example of the missionaries. I especially remember a Mennonite doctor who visited Ethiopia after having served with his church in Vietnam. I was so impressed that he was able to care for people on both sides of that conflict, even those who had been defined by his country as the enemy. Now, whenever I am tempted by violence I try to remember the teaching and example of Jesus, the Anabaptists and those missionaries.

"I also have a conscience against paying military taxes, and once asked my employer not to withhold the military portion of my tax bill. Before this request could be processed, the government took over the company. Now I try to live a very simple lifestyle in order to avoid taxes and witness to my convictions. Please pray for us in Ethiopia that we will be able to follow through on our convictions about nonresistance."

Name withheld on request

Understanding the Arab World

Born in Palestine and raised in Jordan, Elias George had his first contact with Mennonites at the age of nineteen. He had just completed high school when he got his first teaching job at a Mennonite sponsored orphanage in the town of Hebron. Through his contacts at the school, Elias received the opportunity, in 1967, to attend Eastern Mennonite College in Harrisonburg, Virginia.

When he graduated from college, Elias got married and settled in Lancaster County, Pennsylvania. He and his wife Nora have two children, David and Michael.

In November 1990, as the buildup to war in the Persian Gulf intensified, Elias decided to join a Christian Peacemaker Teams (CPT)[1] delegation to the Middle East (Jordan and Iraq). Geographically, it was a trip back home for Elias. His innate understanding of the region provided much of his motivation to participate.

Since Iraq is an Arab country, I thought perhaps I could play a small role in humanizing the U.S. image of the Arabs. Due to the Arab-Israeli conflict, Arabs receive a negative image in the mass media and entertainment industry. Arabs are often portrayed as violent people. They are associated with the Palestine Liberation Organization and equated with terrorists. In many ways, this trip crossed the dividing line between East and West. I thought it was my duty to help people from the West better understand the Arab world.

"For a while I wasn't sure what to think about this opportunity. I didn't approve of Saddam Hussein's actions. I didn't want to defend him, yet I wanted to improve Americans' understanding of Iraq and the Arab world. It was a test of faith for me. The atmosphere was tense. I said to myself, 'I'm a Mennonite, but do I really believe in peacemaking?'

"The people we met in Iraq were genuinely friendly. They wanted peace and feared what would happen to them in war. When we visited the University of Baghdad, I sensed that the students were living by their dreams. They wanted to build up their country and serve the Arab world.

"When talking about the crisis, ordinary Iraqis did not use violent language about America. They frequently said that 'this is a problem between Arab brothers.' I sensed that the Iraqis went into Kuwait, but didn't know how to get back out.

"I was very moved by our reception at the Christian church in Baghdad. We went to the church service unannounced. It was filled with worshipers. We were immediately received very warmly by the priest, who affirmed the purpose of our trip. He told us about a three-day conference for peace which the Christian churches in Iraq were planning in the city of Babylon. Unfortunately, the native church in the Middle East has long been overshadowed by all the political conflicts taking place in that region."

Elias's fluency in Arabic and English put him in great demand as a translator, since there were numerous peace delegations in Baghdad at the time of the CPT visit. One such request for his services caused Elias some anxious moments.

During a period of free time after lunch one day, Elias and several of the team members were relaxing in their room. Suddenly, a member of the Iraqi friendship organization which hosted the CPT team burst into the room and spoke to Elias in Arabic, "Get up! Get up! The revolution is here!"

"He scared me," says Elias. "My heart started beating faster, and I began to worry. What could he mean, 'the revolution is here'? I didn't know what to do. I didn't want to alarm my colleagues, so I didn't say anything to them. I looked at my clothes and said something about changing them, but our host said, 'No, no, you look fine the way you are. Let's go, the revolution is here.'

"In Arab culture, sometimes it shows a lack of trust if you ask too many questions, so I just made up my mind to commit myself. I didn't ask any questions even though I had a million of them spinning in my head.

"We left our building and walked a short distance to another building in the compound. I was escorted through the door, and there to greet me was a journalist from the newspaper, The Revolution. I was so relieved. My job was to translate for the German peace delegation, which I did with pleasure."

Elias feels very positive about the CPT visit to Iraq, and about the strong interest in his trip from the Lancaster community upon his return. The war which followed in January and February, however, was a deep disappointment.

"I cried many times while I watched the bombing of Baghdad. It is a city I came to know. We had spent many of our evenings at the Rashid Hotel. I thought about the people I had met and the places I had been. I found myself praying a lot. I couldn't do much else.

"It hurt to see another Arab country being destroyed. In no way did I approve of Hussein's invasion of Kuwait, but I sensed that the Iraqi people and government wanted a peaceful resolution. If Iraq would have been recognized as an equal, the problem could have been solved peacefully.

"War is a terrible thing. We often prayed as a family around the supper table. 'We submit this matter into your hands, O God. Show yourself to the leaders of the United States and Iraq in order that lives might be saved.'

"My family in Jordan was fearful through all of this. We had lost everything during the war in 1948. We had lost our land and home in Lydda. I was told that my family and others feared an Israeli invasion of Jordan during the Persian Gulf war. They are relieved that the war is over, but disappointed that once again Arabs have been defeated."

As Elias reflects on his effort at peacemaking with Christian Peacemaker Teams, he notes that it has profoundly touched his own life. "This is the first time that I have found myself genuinely believing in peace as the will of the Lord. Since this trip, I am at peace with myself. I went thousands of miles to help bring peace to the world, so now I have to find a way to be at peace with the people around me. I now see reconciliation and conflict resolution as a way of life. I want to live this way as much as I can.

"When you take such a public step, you have to try to live up to it. I could no longer keep my thoughts secret. By going to Iraq on a peace mission, I publicly declared, 'This is me.' I only wish I had done this kind of thing earlier. Our church work and witness would be stronger if we all took this kind of public stand."

It Has to be Perfect
Because It's for Missiles

In 1968, the Wenger* family was busy. Paul was completing a Ph.D. program in American history while his wife, Sarah, taught job skills to handicapped adults. Her job was the primary source of income for the family of six children.

Unknown to Sarah, an ethical dilemma awaited her on the job which would threaten the financial stability of the family. The workshop for handicapped adults had received a contract from the government for the assembly of components for missiles.

Sarah found out about it one day while she was teaching several of the workers how to assemble a small piece of hardware. The director of the workshop happened by and commented, "It has to be perfect, because it's for missiles." Sarah responded immediately, "This pacifist doesn't believe in making weapons for war."

In addition to deeply held religious convictions against participation in warfare, Sarah viewed the issue in a very practical way. "It just didn't make any sense for me to teach handicapped persons to make weapons which would only cause more persons to become handicapped."

Sarah and her family agreed that she should not get involved in the contract, so she took her concerns to the director of the workshop, and to another Mennonite employee who happened to be her Sunday School teacher. She thought perhaps she could be reassigned to another part of the workshop.

The director was understanding of Sarah's concerns, but indicated that the contract was very important to the financial viability of the workshop. He saw no purpose in declining the contract, since it would simply be done by someone else down the street.

Sarah's Sunday School teacher, a supervisor in another section

* Names are fictitious

---

of the workshop, did not see any problem with the contract, and spoke to the ministers at church about the issue. When one of the ministers met with Sarah, he was troubled by her reluctance to continue her employment. He asked her how strong her convictions would be if the Russians sent planes to bomb America.

The director of the workshop discussed Sarah's concerns with the board of directors. The board felt that if she did not want to work with the missile contract, she should be dismissed. Sarah left immediately. The director gave her a glowing recommendation in the hope that it would help her secure another job.

The family was fully aware of the negative financial consequences of this decision. Sarah remembers it this way: "We had some fears, but it all happened so quickly, there was no time to arrange other employment before I left my job. The choice was clear, and I never had any second thoughts."

After a few weeks, both pastors came to see Sarah individually, and expressed support for the position she had taken. The assistant pastor was instrumental in helping her find other employment just a few weeks later.

From the Gang to the Pulpit

Louis Samudio was born in Houston, Texas, and moved with his family to Los Angeles, California when he was five years old. Louis was the second youngest child in a family of eight children. His father worked at Ford Motor Company and his mother cared for the children and took care of the many tasks at home.

Louis' life story moves from gang warfare and drugs to the pulpit of a Mennonite Brethren Church in Los Angeles.

I vaguely remember Vacation Bible School in Texas. My mother was the only Christian in her family. She would send us to the church, and I remember doing crafts in Sunday School. At the age of ten, I got baptized at a church in Los Angeles. I don't remember ever making a profession of faith, but I do remember being baptized in a Baptist church.

"When I was nine or ten years old, I started to hang out with kids in the neighborhood. The gang that belonged to our particular area challenged me to join them. I put it off for a little while, but everybody else urged me to join. I had heard some negative things about gangs, but I thought if my friends were in it, it couldn't be that bad. At school, it was a thing of prestige to be a part of the gang. So, I decided to join."

What came next was the introduction to liquor, marijuana, barbiturates, and eventually harder drugs. "We used to steal things together," recalls Louis. "It was another phase of doing things together and having fun.

"We weren't fighting for control of drug traffic at that time—only territory. The interesting thing was that even if we won, we never took over the territory. The reward was only in winning, and being the strongest and fiercest gang. It was proof of manhood. If we won, we would fight again another day, or the fight would resume again in the next generation.

"During the time that I was part of the gang, I had a deepening fear inside, so I got loaded every time before a fight. When we beat up and stabbed people, I felt troubled inside. But there was overwhelming pressure not be called a quitter. I guess that was my 'success.' I was never a quitter. The gang also gave all of us a strong sense of belonging. Quitting the gang and losing that sense of belonging would have been very frightening."

Nonetheless, when Louis was twenty-three years old, he tried to enlist in the military. "I looked at the army as a job, or as a way to get away. I wanted to go to Vietnam. The recruiter just laughed, and said they would take me only when they started to take women and children. My drugs kept me out."

By the age of thirty, Louis had survived reform school, the Juvenile Detention Center, prison, drug addiction and overdoses, and gang fights.

"I had real good jobs along the way," recalls Louis. "I was an apprentice carpenter for three years. I was an apprentice machinist. I worked at Ford Motor Company. But I could never keep the jobs. My addiction would always get in the way.

"My married life was fluctuating the whole time. My wife was hooked on heroin too. When I was in prison, someone else came to live with her. I was real jealous. I used to beat her a lot. I even beat her before I got onto heroin. I had to sleep with a knife for protection from my own wife."

It was at a government narcotic prevention program that Louis met a Christian counselor.

"My counselor used to tell me, 'If you really want to get rid of everything, the Lord can help you.' I knew that he had been a drug addict. He had been a big dealer. I said to myself, "This guy is no different from me. If he can do it, I can do it." I had been convinced that I was going to die a drug addict, but he told me that my problem was not drugs. I was surprised. When I asked him what my problem was, he said, 'Your problem is that you don't have a relationship with God. Doing drugs is just one of the symptoms of your problem.'

"At the time, I thought this counselor was talking about turning me into a person that is a complete square, someone who has no fun at all. But the thought of this counselor kept coming back to me when I was naked in the jail cell, after I had been arrested and beaten up. I was getting tired of my life, so I made a proposition to

God.

"I knew that I would get sick from withdrawal in prison. Without drugs, a person's nervous system comes back to life, and sleep is impossible. Severe cramps are also common. So I said, 'Lord, if you let me sleep, that's all I want. I'll give my life to you because I'm tired of this. I'll do my time, you don't have to take me out of jail.' The next thing I knew, I woke up. I realized that I had slept. That day was strange. The window was open, across the hall. The sun was shining in extra bright, and I got up on top of the bars to see out. When I looked outside, there was a church with a big cross on its side wall. I said, 'Wow! God heard me!'

"I got a Bible, and read and prayed a lot," remembers Louis. "After ten months, I was chosen to go to the Assemblies of God Bible School. My way was paid. It was from Bible School that I was called to go to the Mennonite church."

Louis's job at the Mennonite church was to help with Sunday School work, look after the parsonage, do some song leading, and help the pastor. Within three years, however, the senior pastor of the church resigned. In 1982, after several years of testing and discernment, Louis became the full-time ordained pastor.

Today, Louis is pastor in the same neighborhood where he used to participate in gang violence. "I'm still considered a part of the gang," he notes. "I'm one of the guys that has successfully 'made it.' They still claim me as one of them. Since I survived and now have a position of responsibility, it helps them have hope."

Louis's allegiance to Christ, and his association with Mennonites have given him a new perspective on violence. "When I first became a Christian, I knew that I couldn't continue fighting, but I didn't think about it in its fullness. My introduction to Mennonites was the first time that the teaching of peace and nonresistance came into my thoughts in a significant way. Mennonites have shown me that the gospel provides another way to settle conflict. When I see a situation of violence, I ask myself, 'What would the Lord want?'"

The streets of Los Angeles have not protected Louis from violent confrontations simply because he has found new life in Christ.

"One time before I was a Christian, someone broke into our house. I caught the man and threatened to kill him, but he got away. In the following weeks, I kept looking for him, and one night I found him. He was drunk, so I just pistol whipped him. I told him that I could have killed him, but that I wanted to do it while he was sober. Before I got a chance to meet him again, I got sent to prison. By the time I got out, he was in prison, and we just kept missing each other.

"Meanwhile, I became a Christian and forgot all about some of these old scores. One evening I was walking out of my house to the van when someone called me from a car parked nearby. I walked over to the car and stuck my head into the window. Here was this same man waiting for me with a hatchet!

"I was so surprised. I said, 'Hey, you know I'm sorry, but I'm not into this anymore. The Lord has changed me.'

"He said, 'You're just trying to get out of this.' I said, 'No, man, you need what I have. Let me go get my Bible. Wait right here.'

"I went over to my van to open the back door, because I knew I had a Bible there. I didn't realize it, but the guy got out of his car and followed me. He didn't trust me at all. He thought I was going to go get a gun. Anyway, I got to the van, opened the door, picked up my Bible and turned around. There was this guy right behind me. His hatchet was already raised and on the way down.

"When he saw the Bible in my hand he stopped. I said to him, 'I told you I've changed.' He was overwhelmed. I called other people together and we all prayed for him. Within a couple weeks, he was in a group home seeking treatment. He said he just couldn't get over what happened to him that night. Now he has received the Lord into his life and feels joy once again."

Part of Louis's mission as a pastor is to help gang members find a new allegiance and sense of belonging in Christ. Louis's prior gang activity provides both difficulties and special gifts in accomplishing this task.

"When I see young kids begin to 'dress up' like gang members, I sometimes get the impulse to 'slap them around' a bit. I know that what awaits them is either death or jail. I'd like to wake them up. It is a temptation I have, but only two times have I physically thrown somebody out of my house in frustration. On those occasions, I have had to ask for forgiveness."

Louis explains how, as a Christian, he relates to people who use violence on others. "I know that the persons who use violence are not really the persons they would be if the Lord were inside them. That is my turning point. I try to view everybody the way they would be if the Lord had control of their lives. That helps me respond to them in love.

"Sometimes now I ride along with the cops in the back seat when they make arrests. I wear a clerical collar and am available to talk to anyone that wants to do that.

"We also have gang rallies at the church. We make a special effort to invite the gangs. We go to where they meet and invite them to come to an evening of music or drama. The church is a neutral zone where various gangs can come. One evening the sanctuary of about 150 seats was filled with members of several different gangs. They came in small clusters and sat

down. Everything was fine during the service, and the police were patrolling the area the whole time.

"On this particular night the gangs started getting a little tense on their way out of the church. I had a doorman that night who was a former member of the Mexican mafia. Everybody knew him and didn't want to mess with him. He told them to go straight home, without stopping to mingle. Fortunately they listened and no fights broke out.

"I think kids come to rallies at the church because a lot of them have had experiences with God in their life and they are still searching. Their problems are deep-seated, and we're learning to deal with them better. We tell them that their problems are not gangs and drugs. Their problem is that they don't allow the Lord to show them who they really are.

"Secondly, we realize that pain can live with them for a long time. But this is not a matter of salvation. They have different kinds of wounds, defense mechanisms and addictions. Many of them are trapped."

Today Louis is working with others in his community on a program for gang and drug prevention, called "Clean Breakthrough." This program is organized by "a group of individuals who have had first-hand experience in gang life styles, and are living proof that there can be a clean breakthrough from gangs and drugs."

While Louis is certain about the implications of the gospel in relation to gang violence, he is less sure about the issue of military service.

"To a certain degree, I feel honor and pride about my country. Here I have the freedom of accomplishing what I want to do. I still have a conflict within me regarding military service. There is something important about fighting to maintain the freedom which the Lord has granted us, whether or not the war is just. Military service feels very different from gang violence.

"We do not currently have members in the congregation who are in military service. We discuss this issue with potential new members, but it is not a test of membership. We explain the peace teaching and note that it is the preference of the denomination, but we leave the choice up to the individual."

Despite his own uncertainty on the issue, Louis does try to help young people explore options other than the military.

"I was counseling a young nineteen-year-old man who was going through hard times. His father was an alcoholic, and this man was seeking the military as a way out of his situation. I told him that the military was not the only way out, and that there were a lot of other options available in Christian service. He hasn't joined the military yet.

"I tell young people that we really never know what is going to take place from one minute to the next. We could be at war at any time. I ask them where they would find peace on this question. If push comes to shove, we encourage them to enter a part of the military where they don't have to fight, so that they can maintain a nonresistant stance."

As Louis considers the way of Christ in his community, and the many difficult problems he faces, he draws inspiration from John 8:32, "You will know the truth, and the truth will set you free."

"When I truthfully ask myself what the Holy Spirit is telling me to do, and face the truth with God's grace, I always seem to accomplish victory over particular obstacles. Instead of stumbling stones, obstacles become stepping stones."

Your Honor, I Will Not Be a Soldier

Sam Martin, a Mennonite from Alberta, Canada, made a routine application for conscientious objector status in early 1943. What followed was a nineteen-month odyssey of prison sentences, solitary confinement and poor health which tested Sam's faith and character. Thankfully, few Canadian conscientious objectors had to endure this kind of hardship.

When Sam first received his orders to report for military training, he applied for conscientious objector status. He assumed that he would be assigned to an alternative service work camp like several of his brothers. Seven weeks later, however, he was called before the Mobilization Board in Edmonton for questioning. Despite Sam's explanation of his religious convictions related to peace, and his record of regular attendance at Duchess Mennonite Church, the judge replied, "Martin, you have not convinced me."

Sam's application for CO status was rejected, but he was given a year-long postponement due to his value to the local farming community as a mechanic.

In early March, 1944, Sam's postponement came to an end. Despite attempts to extend the postponement and to restate his convictions as a CO, Sam was ordered to report to the magistrate in Brooks, Alberta. Before the judge, Sam declared, "Your Honor, I will not be a soldier. I am a conscientious objector. Three times I have been told to join the military, but my answer is unchanged. The Scriptures, as I understand them, tell me not to kill."

Sam was charged with refusing to obey a lawful order, commanded to report for military training, and sentenced to thirty days in the provincial jail at Lethbridge. Following that time, Sam was to be handed over to military authorities.

Church leaders tried to intervene, but on May 13 Sam was placed under military control and his name was written on the army's records as a soldier. When Sam refused to wear a military uniform, he was sentenced to twenty-eight days at the Currie Barracks, a prison for soldiers guilty of desertion and disobedience.

Upon his arrival, the Regimental Sergeant Major declared, "You will wear a uniform! I am in charge here, and there has never been a person under my control whom I haven't been able to break! Take off your civilian clothes and put on an army uniform or go naked!"

Sam quietly replied, "Sir, I refuse to serve in the army. I am a conscientious objector, and I will not wear the uniform."

The prison authorities placed Sam in solitary confinement, and took all his clothes from him except his underwear, and turned off the heat in his room. He was placed on a cyclical diet of three days on bread and water, and three days on regular food. His cell, brightly lit up around the clock, had a bucket for a toilet but no bed. He was given a few blankets for nighttime.

Between May and September of 1944, as each of his sentences ended, Sam again refused to wear the uniform, and was sentenced to additional time in prison.

At times, Sam felt overwhelmed by his seemingly endless suffering. Cold, lonely, and miserable, he imagined that he had been forgotten and that no one cared about his plight.

Sam's family and church had not forgotten him. They prayed for him constantly, and wrote letters. At the end of one twenty-one day period, a guard opened Sam's cell door and threw forty-five letters on the floor for Sam to read. Sam was greatly encouraged by this contact with family and friends.

At times Sam questioned the position he had taken regarding military service. But when he read certain Bible passages, he concluded that he had no choice. Verses which had special meaning included Jesus' words, "Love your enemies and pray for your persecutors so you can be children of your heavenly father" (Matthew 5:43-44). "My Kingdom is not of this world. If my Kingdom were of this world then would my servants fight" (John 18:36).

Sam wondered if he had been too adamant in refusing to wear the military uniform. It was, after all, just another form of clothing. His resolve was strengthened when he learned that several Jehovah's Witnesses had accepted the uniform and had been taken to the military training camp. When they refused to participate in training exercises, they were beaten.

Sam also considered serving in the military's Medical and Dental Corps when this became an option in September of 1943. "If I had understood it as absolutely noncombatant then, I believe I would have accepted it," remembers Sam. Even the slightest possibility that he might be expected to engage in combat led Sam to decline this opportunity.

Numerous appeals were made on Sam's behalf, including a petition signed by 140 non-Mennonites who felt Sam's religious freedom had been violated. This effort seemed to have some effect. Sam was examined by a doctor who warned the officials that his health was precarious.

For a total of forty-nine days, Sam had been on a diet of bread and water, without clothes, and without heat in a cell. He had been deeply chilled, lost quite a lot of weight, and become very weak.

Because of the doctor's report, Sam was transferred to the Lethbridge provincial jail where he received better treatment. He was assigned to work as a mechanic, and later became co-manager of the prison farm. He served nearly two-thirds of this eighteen-month sentence before his "industrial leave" on November 8, 1945. On April 12, 1946, Sam was officially discharged from the army.

Reflecting on his experience forty-five years later, Sam notes, "I received an understanding of what it means to be the church. It is much more than an association of people—it is a body. When one member suffers, the whole body suffers."[1]

Legitimate Self-Defense?

Mennonites entered the Ukraine in the late 1700s at the invitation of Catherine the Great. In her search for farmers to settle the vast prairies of South Russia, Catharine promised all foreign settlers that they could live in self-governing colonies and would be exempt from military service. Within 125 years, between 1917 and 1919, the Mennonite colonists faced the chaos and violence created by the Russian civil war. In this personal account, written in September, 1978, Bernhard Dick reflects on their desperate plight and the temptation to form a Self-defense Unit or Selbstschutz *to protect themselves.*

The Soviet government, weak and inexperienced, was completely unable to maintain law and order in the huge Russian empire. Vicious mobs of anarchists moved through the countryside. Robbing and killing, gangs moved about and molested both German and Russian estate owners, factories and mills and then attacked the Mennonite mother and daughter colonies. For half a year we were exposed to the despotism of these bandits. The thought of an emergency Selbstschutz became strong among many Mennonites. Quite often we heard men saying: "To rob my possessions is one thing—but they won't touch my wife or my daughter. Then I'll grab the axe I keep handy for that purpose." The bandits always grabbed the men first, severely torturing them in order to obtain money, gold, silver and other valuables—if such were still available—and then killing them or tying them up. After the bandits had robbed the house, the women were locked up and victimized. And so the idea of a Selbstschutz was nourished and came to fruition.

Then came a short respite. Following the Treaty of Brest-Litovsk, March 3, 1918, signed by Germany and Soviet Russia, the German military occupied the Ukraine and remained there until October, 1918. This was a most welcome period of peace, a breathing space sent by God. Not always and not in all cases was the conduct of these German soldiers commendable and inoffensive, and yet through their courageous, bold actions against the anarchists, the first flickers of the Selbstschutz were fanned among our men into a blazing fire.

Because of the revolutionary unrest in Germany itself, the German military was recalled from Russia and we were now exposed to new terrors at the hands of the Nestor Makhno bandits. The time had come for the establishment and organization of the Selbstschutz.

The die was cast. Robber gangs now surrounded our villages. The German officers who had remained behind, and a few Russian officers who had ample weapons, urged us to act. Hastily, a three-day general conference with regard to this issue was convened in the village of Lichtenau from June 30 till July 2, 1918. I was present, a 23-year-old young man suffering great mental anguish, looking for answers. The vague resolutions passed at this conference did not call for a condemnation of the men who felt compelled to join the Selbstschutz, but at the same time requested that the conscience of the total nonresisters be respected. The decision was left up to the individual. It is deplorable that our leading men at that time could not arrive at a clearer course of action. Whether it was the "Cossack" or the "most welcome German occupation force," or the Selbstschutz, where was our absolute nonresistance if we allowed ourselves to be protected and defended by others?

As I mentioned, when the German troops withdrew, all law and order vanished and things became worse than before. Helpless and defenseless, we were exposed to the horrible reality of an unprecedented, bestial anarchy that expressed the basest human instincts. In our villages and communities there were now two opposing camps. The officers of the White Army in Berdjansk, who were prepared to help us, waited anxiously for more definite answers from the conference and from the Mennonite community in general. The eight Lutheran villages (Prischieb) lying north of the Molotshna were wholly united, and were prepared to join our Selbstschutz, pressing and urging us to make up our minds. Our people vacillated. There were those who considered nonresistance a mere tradition and pointed out how Abraham of old rescued Lot militarily, how David had killed the giant Goliath, how Samson had killed the Philistines. Others advocated a strict nonresistance based on the Word of God of the New Testament, on Jesus' teaching, life, suffering and death as the almighty Son of God.

Then, at special meetings in several villages, the Selbstschutz was organized, often with assistance from the German officers. Those Mennonites who had fled to the villages from their estates outside the colonies affirmed the Selbstschutz. Many of these refugees had not only lost their possessions, but had also witnessed terrible cruelties committed against their loved ones. They were obsessed with thoughts of vengeance. And who could hold this against them? I certainly could not.

Many others thought and felt as I did: "Love your enemies. Bless those who curse you. Do good to those who persecute you." Yet how difficult it was! These latter people had not experienced what the victims of terror had experienced.

The more prosperous farmers were generally more in favor of the Selbstschutz than the landless and the poor Mennonites. Whether there was a significant difference in attitude between the various church groups, I cannot say.

My refusal to take part in the Selbstschutz—here God is my witness—did not spring from cowardice or fear of death but was based on my position of faith with regard to nonresistance and the teachings of Jesus in the ups and downs of life. So we had been taught, and thus we understood Scriptures. Because of this position our forefathers had suffered bloody persecution, and because of this belief the principle of nonresistance was included in the Privilegium (special privileges) granted to us by the Russian government.

In my anguish of mind, I drove to my former teacher of religion, Abram Klassen in Halbstadt, some twenty-five versts (one verst is approximately two thirds of a mile) away. Brother Klassen was an elder of the Mennonite Church. I put before him the questions that weighed heavily on my heart. He said: "Young man, you should not try to jump over a church steeple with your piety. Why don't you begin humbly at home with your beliefs, and in your own surroundings? Wanting to know better than everyone else is not becoming to you, don't you agree?" Feeling humiliated, discouraged and very miserable, I drove home. (Abram Klassen is believed to have died later, because of his faith—after we had left for Canada—in a prison in Melitopol.)

When I got home that day, I hitched two fresh horses to the wagon and drove to Gnadenfeld (about eighteen versts away) to see Sergeant Sonntag, one of the men at the headquarters of the Selbstschutz. I told him also about my mental distress. But this German military man showed absolutely no understanding for my attitude toward nonresistance. In the end, I requested from him something in writing which would allow me to become a medical orderly, but he refused to grant my request.

"Young man, you've shot a rabbit, haven't you?" he asked me.

I answered, "Yes, of course—so?"

"So, what's the difference?" he asked.

"But a man has a soul!" I replied.

Leaning far back in his armchair, he laughed and laughed, repeating my words over and over again: "Man has a soul! Man has a soul!"

I drove home even more discouraged than before. There was great excitement in the village. I was told that Brother Jakob Reimer from Rueckenau had been invited to speak in our meetinghouse that evening in order to give us a definitive, clarifying answer concerning the problem of the Selbstschutz. Men from several villages gathered at the meetinghouse. I was certain that this highly respected man of God would support us believers. Exactly the opposite happened. Referring to many biblical passages from the Old Testament, where Jehovah God commanded the Israelites and Joshua to destroy all seven pagan nations of Canaan—including men, women and children—Brother Jakob Reimer supported the organization of a Selbstschutz.

That night I knelt beside my bed, praying and weeping. And the Lord was gracious to me and stood by me. I remained firm in my offer to serve as a medical orderly and no more. People in the village recognized my sincerity and sympathized with me. They punished my brother Johann, who also remained nonresistant, by appointing him night watchman in our village for a considerable period of time. This was a miserable contradiction in itself, to send a nonresistant Mennonite without a weapon to stand guard in those dangerous times!

Even though the bandits were of superior strength, our Selbstschutz kept them at bay for three months—December, 1918 to March 6, 1919. The gangs allied themselves with the Bolshevik troops from the north—a fact which our people did not know at the time—and the Selbstschutz had to fight, in the end, against a vastly superior force. The "self-defensers" were consequently forced to abandon everything and to fall back into a slow retreat.

Where I was located, our people held positions in three lines. In

the front line they operated with machine guns. One day, a lieutenant suddenly came running from the rear line, very excited, and
shouted: "I need a volunteer! This cartridge belt has to be taken to
the front line right now!" No one volunteered. It was only hours
before the final collapse, and the enemy was beginning to attack
front and center. Suddenly something came over me. After a fast
and fervent prayer I volunteered: "Give it to me, please!" God only
knows how many rifle barrels were levelled at me. In fear of death
I ran as fast as I possibly could. Bullets whistled all around me and
hit the ground left and right. At least three times I threw myself to
the ground, only to jump up after a few minutes and continue
running. I got there and back again without mishap. To this day I
believe God protected me.

My action was, of course, wrong and contrary to my nonresistant
position. With that cartridge belt there were perhaps more persons
killed in half an hour than with all the rifle shots of the individual
"self-defensers." I would like to state in my own defense, however,
that anyone who has not been in a similar situation should be
cautious in passing judgment.

The retreat that night is difficult to describe. Entire villages
left everything behind and fled in wagons just to save their lives.
Many refugees were hacked to pieces by the bandits on the way.
Some of our people courageously and selflessly walked directly into
the lion's den—the headquarters of the Reds in Gross Tokmak—and
pleaded for mercy. They solemnly declared that we had founded the
Selbstschutz for protection against the bandits only, and that we
did not know that in the end we were fighting against government
troops. This explanation lessened the punishment.

The bandits now flooded our villages and furiously robbed, killed
and raped—their leaders had given them three days' leave for that
purpose. The northern villages, which were located close to the
Russian settlements, were affected more than others. Hostages
were taken according to the size of the villages and confined with
threats of execution if within a specified period of time the villages
failed to deliver a certain number of rifles, sabres, hand grenades
and other weapons. My father, who had been the mayor of our
village, was arrested first, and with him three others. Difficult weeks
followed! Many of the former "self-defensers" fled together with the
Russian White generals to the Crimea and took their rifles with
them. This is why it was difficult to deliver the required quota of
weapons. We searched feverishly for rifles and munition! To save

the captured hostages, people combed through wells, cellars, streams, and chaff bins in search of weapons. Periodically, some of the hostages were shot, especially in the upper villages.

As the civil war continued and the fronts between the Whites and the Reds swayed back and forth, our villages suffered greatly. Some villages changed hands from seven to ten times—and because of our former Selbstschutz activities, the Reds now considered us their enemies.

There are those who claim to this day that without the Selbst-schutz things would have been much worse. I refrain from express-ing an opinion on this matter. One thing is clear: for the individual reader of this account, one who was perhaps born decades after those terrible events, it is no doubt impossible to understand fully our situation at that time, to empathize with the anguish of the believers in nonresistance, and to judge this matter fairly.

May God Almighty be gracious to all of us and preserve us and all other countries from similar tragedies! May the Lord's reign of peace begin soon, in which swords shall be beaten into plowshares and spears into pruning hooks. Then delight and joy shall fill our hearts forever and ever. May God grant us this![1]

Through the Women's Eyes

In 1985, Brenda Stoltzfus began an assignment with Mennonite Central Committee in Olongapo City, Philippines, exploring how MCC might respond to the presence of the U.S. military bases, particularly to the Filipina women who worked as prostitutes. After nearly a year in this assignment, Brenda wrote the following reflections.

We, the American public, are asked regularly by President Reagan to support U.S. military build-up. We are told our military strength is significant to worldwide peace. We seldom hear about the social costs to the countries whose land we use to maintain that strength. The Philippines is one such country. Olongapo, a city on the northern island of Luzon, is just outside Subic naval base, the largest U.S. naval installation outside U.S. territory.

The stories of Olongapo have become a deep part of me. The stories I know best are the stories of the hospitality women (prostitutes) who service the sailors coming into Subic Bay. These are the women who have become my friends and whose pain I share.

Out of a population of about 300,000 in Olongapo City, roughly 17,000 to 20,000 women are registered prostitutes, meaning they are employed in a bar or massage parlor, and are thus "legal." Streetwalkers are women who are not employed in a bar, meaning they are illegal and subject to arrest. U.S. sailors leaving the main gate of Subic base walk directly onto the strip—the main street of Olongapo lined with bars, massage parlors, hotels, and souvenir or T-shirt shops.

Prostitution is truly institutionalized in Olongapo. Women are employed as cashiers, waitresses, a-go-go dancers and entertainers. Waitresses generally receive no salary; they depend almost entirely on commissions. Commissions are earned on Ladies Drinks and Bar Fines. A Ladies Drink is a mixed drink bought by the sailor for the woman with the expectation she will sit and talk to him. He pays the bar about $1.50, of which she receives about fifty cents. A Bar Fine is the money a sailor pays to take the woman out of the bar—generally meaning sexual intercourse, although not always. He pays the bar between fifteen and sixty dollars, depending on the bar. She generally receives less than half. Women working in bars and massage parlors are required to have VD (venereal disease) smears every other week at a Social Hygiene Clinic which is given financial and technical assistance by the U.S. Navy. Bars are owned by Filipino and Chinese business persons and American ex-Navy men married to Filipinas.

Olongapo is a subculture full of misperceptions, illusions and misplaced assumptions. The women are seeking a better life—not only adequate food and material well-being, but also good family relationships. The sailors are also caught in a system. They are often young, far away from home and under tremendous peer pressure. Many assume the women have chosen this life-style in the true sense of the word "choice." The U.S. Navy assumes the sailors need an outlet for their sexual drives after being at sea several months. Providing "Rest and Recreation" in cahoots with the local city government, they believe, is better than massive rape.

Neng and Vicky are friends of mine. They are full of life. We have had many good times together.

I went to their bar late one afternoon. Neither was there and the women told me Neng had gone to the hospital and Vicky was there with her. I took off immediately for the hospital, my mind reeling. What could be wrong?

Neng did not go on Bar Fines, but had been raped about a month before. She was pressured into going on a Bar Fine by her supervisor and agreed on the condition they not go to a hotel. She took him to her house because she knew her roommates were there. When she went into her bedroom to get something he followed her in, closed and locked the door, and raped her. She had to be taken to the hospital where she was given six stitches. The Shore Patrol made the sailor pay her hospital bills and an additional fifty dollars. They asked her if she wanted to marry him. Needless to say, she did not.

I arrived at the hospital and found Neng, Vicky and Neng's younger sisters all there. Vicky told me that Neng was there because of an infection, probably a result of the rape. Neng lay in her hospital bed, weak but improving.

After the others left the hospital, I sat stroking Neng's hair as she drifted off to sleep. I thought about everything she had been through before the age of twenty-one. Several years before, in her own province, she hid in a church to escape being forced to become a mistress to her boss. Later, she was taken to Manila by a recruiter, and found herself in a prostitution house where, because she did not want to be a prostitute, she washed clothes and cleaned during the day and had her feet chained together at night so she could not escape. But she did escape, and ended up in Olongapo sending money home regularly to help support her family. And now this.

I thought of myself, graduating from a Mennonite college in Indiana at twenty-one, full of dreams for the future and pleasant memories of the past. How different our lives had been, seemingly only by fate. I was born into a middle class Mennonite family in the States; she, into a poor farming family in Samar, one of the most impoverished islands in the Philippines. Had I been born into her family, I could be in the same situation.

Since I was born where I was, what should my role be as a friend to Neng and to all the other friends I now have here? It is a question I carry with me constantly. My life was much easier before I gained these friends, and yet my life is much richer for knowing them. How my commitment to them works itself out I have not yet discovered. I can only hope we will be able to discover it, in some measure, together.

What does our much-used language of "bringing about the Kingdom of God" mean in a situation where our country is directly, as well as indirectly, responsible for so much pain and injustice—not only with regard to prostitution, but also the presence of the bases in the Philippines and their effect on the economy and political situation? What is our understanding or concept of sin? Does it blame the victim or does it recognize our own dirty hands—our own part in the international community? How then do we live and love in the global community?

I Don't Know Who's Going to Hire You!

Civilian Public Service (CPS) was organized in the United States during the buildup to World War II. The Historic Peace Churches (Mennonites, Quakers and Brethren) sought to avoid a recurrence of the harsh treatment given to conscientious objectors (COs) during World War I. They negotiated with the U.S. government for a program in which COs could engage in alternative service assignments and thereby contribute to the national welfare. Although the history and circumstances were different in Canada, many Mennonite young men there participated in a similar alternative service program in World War II.

Supported by the Peace Churches themselves, CPS men (and a few volunteer women) worked at an immense variety of projects. They built roads, fought forest fires, constructed dams, planted trees, built contour strips on farms, served as guinea pigs for medical and scientific research, built sanitary facilities for hookworm-ridden communities and cared for the mentally ill and juvenile delinquents. In the United States, some 12,000 men participated in CPS—40% of Mennonite or Amish background.[1] In Canada, some 7,500 Mennonite men worked in alternative service assignments.[2]

Mervin J. Hostetler participated in the U.S. Civilian Public Service program in World War II. During his 3-year assignment (1942-1945), he helped to install privies as part of a hookworm control program in Florida, worked at soil conservation in Virginia and served on a mental hospital ward in Pennsylvania.

"CPS was not a voluntary service," Mervin notes. "We were inducted into it according to law, by Selective Service, to do 'work of national importance.' We were not draft dodgers. There were times, of course, while looking down a post hole in Grottoes,

Virginia, or sweating at the bottom of a privy pit in Polk County, Florida—a lot of my CPS experience had to do with holes in the ground—there were times when I felt persecuted. But when I look at the whole picture, I have the satisfaction that I participated in something that had significance beyond the value of the work accomplished.

"Objectors to war were not heroes in World War II. National political figures did not speak against U.S. participation in the war in those days. Most church people were against the objector. We were told we were not welcome in some churches near the camps. An occasional driver seeing us on a sidewalk in town felt free to drive his car off the street and pass us on the sidewalk with a near miss. Chain gangs of convicts working along the road felt sufficiently superior to yell 'CO' and other less complimentary epithets as we rode by in an open project truck. The evidence of rejection by society in general is formidable to anyone. And no amount of persuasion could convince most people that we were anything but disloyal, cowardly citizens.

"One aspect of our testimony did get through with some force. We gave our service without pay. People could not correlate this with all the other conclusions they had formed concerning us. This fact sold the program to the government officials originally, and never ceased to amaze those who worked closely with us."

Nonetheless, society's rejection of CPS workers continued, and did not end with the war. Mervin continued to feel its impact as he finished his education and then sought employmemt.

"In the engineering college of a large university almost all of my classmates were attending under provisions of the GI Bill. So, for example, when we were required to buy a second pair of expensive safety goggles for a welding laboratory because the specification was changed before the first pair was used, no one objected. No one, of course, except me. I wanted to trade in the unused pair.

"Why? Turn it in on the GI Bill!"

"I'm not under the GI Bill."

"Why aren't you?"

The torrent of abusive language that followed my answer almost makes me cower today. I bought the second pair.

"Three years after the war's end I was seeking employment. Nearly every application had a question about military experience. My answer, in most instances, eliminated a follow-up interview. I was finally able to secure an interview with an engineering executive of a large corporation who asked few questions beforehand. I shall never forget the abruptness with which he concluded the session when the subject of past military service came up. He simply got up from behind his desk, walked over and opened his office door, looked at me with a condescending smile, and said, 'I don't know who's going to hire you. Good luck!'

"It has not been possible to entirely shed the effects of these experiences. I am still cautious about speaking of my 'military experience' in World War II. I wish it were not so. Should not Christians be conditioned to receive rejection?

"I would not want to give up the experience of those years if I could. Would I repeat them? Sometimes I almost wish I were forced to the choice again. Maybe our cultural and religious training makes us feel more worthwhile if we make some sacrifice because of what we believe."[3]

Preaching to the Soldiers

Miguel* is a Mennonite pastor in the country of Honduras, where military conscription can take place unexpectedly and by force, in the marketplace or other public places.

As far as Miguel was concerned, he was making another routine trip from La Ceiba back to his home town. He was taking a course at SEMILLA, a Mennonite supported seminary which provides training for pastors and church workers throughout Central America. As usual, he traveled by bus. On this particular day, however, the bus was stopped by a group of soldiers who were conducting on-the-spot recruitment for military service.

All the young persons were ordered off the bus. Much to Miguel's dismay, he was the only one of draftable age, and all the attention was focused on him. Miguel showed the soldiers his identification papers, including his pastoral license. When his papers were returned, he collected his belongings and began to board the bus, only to hear the words, "Where do you think you are going? You are recruited!"

Miguel explained his convictions, stating that as a Christian he could not participate in military service. In addition, he appealed to the fact that Honduran law exempted pastors and other religious workers from military service. The soldiers scowled and asked Miguel just how he thought he could oppose them.

Miguel told the soldiers that he was not trying to oppose them. He only wished to give his point of view, and to explain that his work and his conscience did not permit him to engage in military-related activity.

The longer Miguel talked, the more suspicious the soldiers became. They accused him of being a subversive. They looked at Miguel's books and materials from seminary, and asked questions

* Fictitious name

about other aspects of his life.

Finally, Miguel tried to board the bus a second time. The soldiers' suspicion turned to anger, and they grabbed Miguel and beat him severely. Miguel was thrown into another vehicle, and taken to the military barracks. His condition was such that he required medical treatment, and was ordered to rest for fifteen days.

At the barracks, Miguel was questioned further by the lieutenants. "How is it that being a good Honduran, a religious person, and given that the Bible says that one must obey the authorities, you are resisting?"

Miguel explained that there are many ways to serve one's country. Noting that unemployment and drug addiction are problems in Honduras, Miguel explained that he and his congregation are addressing some of these issues. Through the establishment of a sewing cooperative, for example, his congregation helped to employ five people. The lieutenants said that this was merely a matter of work, not of serving one's country.

Since Miguel had identified himself as a pastor, the lieutenants gave Miguel the responsibility of preaching to the soldiers. On one occasion when the majority of the soldiers were present, Miguel decided to share his convictions about military service. "We have been recruited supposedly for training for war," Miguel said. "But we should never have faith in war preparations as a way to achieve peace. Rather, peace is achieved through fearing God and loving other persons."

The sermon lasted only five minutes. Miguel's superiors asked him to stop, and he was called in for further questioning. Once again the questions focused on Miguel's work and seminary studies. He was somewhat nervous when the lieutenant in charge asked Miguel to show him his books from seminary, "What I feared the most was that he would be able to understand the book The Politics of Jesus,[1] by John Howard Yoder. But he looked it over and didn't understand it."

Following his initial beating when he was recruited, Miguel was not harmed or mistreated at the military barracks. The lieutenants even suggested to Miguel that he could serve a positive role at the barracks. "Here you can preach, too," they said. "Since you are a student and can have debates with us, you could move up quickly." Miguel replied that he sustained his objection to military service, and that he ought not continue serving in the present way.

One afternoon Miguel was asked to put on a green soldier's

uniform. "I struggled with myself as never before. Should I put on the uniform or not? For a moment I felt that I shouldn't do it. I remember a soldier looking at me and saying, 'Hey, you, why are you crying?' I wasn't aware that I was crying, so I responded, 'I'm not crying about anything.' He said to me, 'So what are you thinking, you don't want to put on the uniform?' But he was already prejudiced against me because he was one of those who had grabbed me.

"It was a tough experience. I still didn't get dressed and all the others did. When I tried to put it on, my conscience wouldn't permit me to do it. But a sergeant came to me very angrily, quite violently. So I put on the uniform, but I remember that after doing it I felt that I was failing my faith. Brothers and sisters, this is ugly—to struggle against oneself."

Miguel's family and church community worked hard to secure his release, but received no response. Meanwhile, Miguel was not well, and asked repeatedly to see a medical doctor. Finally he was examined and placed in a group with others who were ill. Much to his surprise and joy, he received his release papers, and was sent home.

Entering Samaria

From 1987-1991, André Gingerich Stoner, an American Mennonite, worked in the Hunsruck area of Germany, which is home to nearly sixty United States, German, and French military installations. The purpose of his work was to assist German peace groups in opening up meaningful dialogue with American soldiers on questions of Christian discipleship and nonviolence.

In fall 1987 the Hunsruck peace initiative sponsored a week-long blockade of the cruise missile base. The purpose was to urge greater resolve in moving towards an INF (Intermediate Nuclear Force) treaty and to protest plans for further military bases in the region. People prepared to face arrest sat down together on one of the four entrance roads leading into the base. Sometimes the military simply closed the gate and redirected traffic. At other times the blockaders were arrested by the German police.

After spending an afternoon with the protesters, I decided to walk alone to another gate to discuss day's events with some of the American guards. When I approached the guard post a short man with dark, distrustful eyes met me. He seemed to be hiding behind his metallic blue Air Force coat and beret. I greeted him in English and was met by silence. He clutched his M-16 and stared at me coldly. I returned his gaze. I couldn't tell if it was fear or hate or anger I was up against.

After a few moments he asked curtly, "What do you want?"

"I'm with the blockaders at the other gate," I offered. "I wanted to explain to you who we are and why we're here."

"I don't want to talk," he snapped.

Not knowing what else to do I decided to stand there silently and pray. "Even if we do not exchange a single word," I thought, "after half an hour maybe he will have grown accustomed to me and will have realized that I mean no harm." So I stood in silence.

About fifteen minutes later, he suddenly approached me and

---

almost breathlessly began asking questions: "Who are you? What do you want? How do I know you're not terrorists? Does it do any good to protest? What do the Germans think of us?"

A few minutes earlier, just for the fun of it, several blockaders had swooped past the gate with brooms acting like crazy witches. This guard, Greg, was agitated and could not understand this. The only purpose he saw was to provoke him. I shared my own discomfort with the attitudes and prejudices of some members of the peace movement towards GIs (American soldiers), and Greg began sharing his own questions and uncertainties.

"I'm just doing my job," he kept repeating. "What do you want from me? You should talk to the politicians." He claimed to be a policeman, not a soldier. It was all the same, he insisted, whether he walked a beat in some city or protected government property.

He relaxed considerably when I told him that we oppose the weapons and what they stand for, but not him or his friends. Greg thought everyone in the peace movement got orders and pay directly from the Soviet Union. He believed the labels "communist," "terrorist," "Green" and "peace movement" were interchangeable. He was impressed to learn that the blockade was announced publicly, that blockaders were asked to sign a pledge of nonviolence and that many were Christians. I told him decisions are made democratically in small affinity groups where members are accountable to each other. "I never knew any of that!" he exclaimed.

We had talked for about thirty minutes when an Air Force police car rolled up and called Greg over. He returned and looked at me helplessly, "I just got chewed out for talking to you."

"I'll make it easy for you and leave," I responded. Greg nodded. In a short time this guard's perspective began to change: We shook hands and said goodbye, friends.[1]

An Individual Witness

Keisuke Matsumoto, a member of the Kamishihoro Mennonite Church in Hokkaido, Japan, describes his journey toward peace and his witness regarding Japan's military taxes:

I was born in Tokyo and grew up there until I was twelve years old. Then it was World War II. We suffered many American air attacks—some of my good friends and relatives were killed or injured by American bombings. I hated America very much at that time. But after Jesus Christ came into my mind, that hate gradually died away. I also became aware that Japan created trouble for other peoples, particularly in Asia.

I would like to walk as a disciple of Jesus and thereby redeem the deaths of my friends and relatives. One of my efforts at discipleship is to try to refuse to pay Japan's army tax. The government tax is withheld every year from salaried men. In 1990, the military received six percent of the tax. This percentage is gradually increasing every year.

So every year on March 10, I visit the tax office and ask that they pay back my army tax. This is the anniversary of the largest American air attack on Tokyo, which killed 85,000 citizens in one night. My aunt was one of those who died in the carpet bombing. At the time, I swore revenge.

At the tax office, I go to the front desk and read my statement explaining why I ask to have my army tax returned. My request usually includes four parts. The first is based on the Japanese constitution, which prohibits the possession of armaments. The second is based on Christianity. In the third part I mention a current issue, which in 1991 was the Persian Gulf war. Finally, I make a proposal for founding a peace tax instead of the army tax. At this time I usually ask to meet the press representatives.

The next day my action is reported in the papers. Usually I get both encouragement and opposition, sometimes threatening letters

---

or phone calls.

About two months after my appeal at the tax office, I receive a notice stating: "Your tax is already accepted." I have not taken this matter before the court because it takes too much time and money. My action is just a witness, although I am supporting another group that is struggling with the court.

Although the Japan Mennonite Christian Conference in Hokkaido has no official position on paying army taxes, young Mennonite members have gone along with me when I read my statement at the tax office. This is quite helpful and gives me encouragement. Some young Mennonites have also joined me in my statement, but only occasionally. I think many of the Mennonite church members agree with my idea and pray for me.

I have been giving this witness for seven years now and only two years remain before my retirement. Since I work for a town government, my situation has not been easy. But I can continue with the help of God and some friends in my section who love peace. I would like to find a successor in my church group who is willing to try this witness despite the sacrifice it could mean for their promotion at work. [1]

We Don't Quote Estimates on Military Jobs

Ervin Steinman is the manager of Riverside Brass, a family-owned business in Ontario, Canada. The business is a sand-casting foundry which produces a variety of unfinished raw castings made of aluminum and copper alloys. The company currently employs 45 people, down from a peak of 70 employees several years ago. Given the small, closely-held nature of the business, management and employees have generally agreed on operating philosophy and ethical issues. As this story indicates, however, Riverside Brass has had some difficult choices to make.

In 1969, Riverside Brass bought an expensive shot-blast machine for cleaning raw castings. A heat treating company in Kitchener learned of this, and called to say they had occasional need for just such a machine. One of the company's jobs involved cleaning the scales off one million pieces of steel. Ervin agreed to take the job. Riverside Brass was not using the shot blast machine to capacity, and the extra work would help the machine pay for itself.

About half way through the contract, the Kitchener firm's owner mentioned that a government inspector might stop in to observe the work. It was then that Ervin asked just exactly what the pieces of steel were. He was informed that they were canteen cup handles for the U.S. Army. In that moment, Ervin decided to always ask about the nature of a job before taking on a contract, no matter how harmless it sounded. Riverside Brass fulfilled the second half of its commitment, but refused to do anything more for that company.

Ervin points out that this incident was near the beginning of his business career when he was still full of idealism. While the contract's military connections bothered him, the fact that he, a Canadian, was contributing to the U.S. military effort bothered him even more.

Riverside's policy of no military contracts has been frequently tested. "I often get blueprints for estimates on a job, which say down in the corner, U.S. Army," explains Ervin. "We simply don't quote an estimate on such jobs. If we're being asked in person to take on a military contract, we explain our no-military-contracts policy.

"I've never had an uncomfortable response to this policy. People just seem to understand. Perhaps a policy like ours is not so unusual in the industry after all." He noted that there is a much lower demand for military items now than there was in the early '70s when the Vietnam War was in progress.

Nevertheless, in early 1990, Ervin's son-in-law and partner, Lynn Jantzi, found himself walking away from potential business because of its military connections. Unlike former times, Riverside Brass needed to be more aggressive in seeking out work. One of Lynn's jobs was to scan the trade magazines for potential clients who needed castings, and then make a visit to drum up business. Lynn had set up an appointment with a company in Trenton/Belleville, Ontario. When he entered the business' lobby, however, he found it filled with armaments on display. Although Riverside could have used the work, Lynn politely informed his contact of Riverside's no-military-contracts policy and left.

"I'm comfortable with the policy," Lynn commented. "It makes it easier for me to follow my own convictions. I would find it much harder if my father-in-law accepted military contracts."

The ethical choices have not always been clear, Ervin notes. "How do you know if something is 'military' or not?" He struggles to separate the grays from the blacks and whites.

Earlier in the business' history," Ervin points out, "declining military work didn't cause Riverside Brass a major loss. There was always plenty of work. Over the past few years, however, we've allowed our work force to decrease through attrition, rather than take on military work. Actually needing to lay workers off would take more soul searching. It seems that the East-West confrontation is lessening. If the U.S. scales down its military, it will drastically affect our kind of business. Companies that formerly did military work will go after the kind of contracts we have been doing all along. If, however, the military expands, some companies really go for their big dollars and we have a better crack at what's left."

Military contract offers come in many ways, and it takes a certain amount of vigilance to spot them. In late 1990, Riverside Brass was given the opportunity to bid on forty-five thousand oval shaped rings. This was not a big job, and as is often the case, it came as a subcontract. Later, Riverside Brass realized that the rings were for body bags being purchased by the Canadian Army for use in the event of a war in the Middle East. Noted Ervin, "I'm not sure if we made a price quote on it or not, but it's the kind of decision that you think about longer when work is hard to find."

Ervin makes his decisions regarding military contracts in the context of a community. "My faith has always been heavily predicated upon what the church decides as a body. In a sense, I don't have a choice on military matters, if I want to be a member of the church. Growing up in the Amish tradition, you were either in or out. I remember in World War II, my older brothers went to conscientious objector camps, but the few church members who weren't COs were very marginalized. Non-COs were disciplined by the church. It was the same with any other form of removing yourself from the fellowship. If someone didn't show up at a barnraising or a funeral, if someone didn't contribute money to a need, if someone went to war, they had obviously removed themselves from fellowship.

"I don't recall talking with fellow church members about this particular policy on military production. I guess I was more alone in facing the military question, but I felt supported by the church. I was a member of Mennonite Economic Development Associates in its earlier forms, and found help and reinforcement on this issue there. It always seemed to me that there was really no question on this. I understood my church's stance on participation in war, so for me my policy just naturally followed out of that church stance."

Getting A "Valve Job" from the U.S. Military

Ruth Yoder Stauffer worked as a nurse in Vietnam from 1966-1972, under the auspices of Mennonite Central Committee. As a U.S. citizen working in a war-torn country in which the U.S. was a principal combatant, Ruth struggled with questions of faith and identity.

Her story begins in Nha Trang, Vietnam, in the fall of 1969 at the end of her first term of service. Knowing that she would not be returning to work in Nha Trang that following year, Ruth wanted to discuss her deep concerns about the war with her interpreter.

Before I left, I wanted to make one last attempt to communicate with Tuyet,* my interpreter, about my viewpoint, as a Mennonite, of the whole situation in Vietnam. We didn't talk a lot, but I tried to tell her how I understood Jesus' teaching about loving our enemies, and how I could not reconcile that with the American military presence in Vietnam.

Tuyet thought a little while, then looked right at me and said, "Ruth, do you know what that position would mean to me and my family? It would likely mean that we couldn't go to church. It would likely mean that my nephews and nieces would be raised under a communist regime. Do you think that this is God's will for us? Would you like for your family to live under communism?"

Well, that hit where it hurt, and I could not forget it. When I was on home leave, I listened to well-meaning Mennonites say, "Well, you know I don't believe in killing anybody, but you've got to stop the communists somewhere." These people could afford the luxury of not believing in killing anybody, while having the communists stopped for them.

I struggled with this during my home leave. I finally came to the

*Fictitious name

conclusion that I needed to either believe in war as an answer to some problems, or not believe in it at all—and depend on what I understood the New Testament to say.

The fall of 1969 was the beginning of my second three year term with MCC in Vietnam. I worked in a health clinic in Saigon under the auspices of the Eastern Mennonite Board of Missions in Saigon. This was in an area near the Gia Dinh Mennonite Church, a needy area which had been hit hard by the Tet offensive in early spring, and by a second military strike a couple months later. The clinic was one of the ways the local church responded to the needs of people living in the area.

When I had left Nha Trang, there were at least ten thousand American military personnel in and around the city. Unless I opened my mouth to speak some Vietnamese, it was assumed that I, an American female on the street, was with the American military or with the U.S. government's Agency for International Development program. This was troubling to me as a Mennonite who hoped to make some small statement that war was not the answer to problems. The Vietnamese Protestant Church with whom we worked did not share our feelings about peace and war either, so we needed to sort out who we really were.

Now I was working in a Mennonite-sponsored clinic in Saigon, just a couple miles from the large U.S. Army Third Field Hospital, one of the best hospitals in Vietnam. The doctor with whom I worked at the clinic was Dr. Smith-T, a Presbyterian woman who had come to Vietnam under the auspices of Vietnam Christian Service.[1] She kept up to date with her medical practice and certifications through the medical meetings at the Army's Third Field Hospital, a place where she was well known and respected.

The Army hospital was staffed by American doctors, nurses, and specialists. Since Dr. Smith-T knew some of the Army doctors on a first name basis, she could easily make referrals for our Vietnamese patients. She could simply write a note, "Dear Bob, I think this boy needs a valve job. What do you think? Joanne." And with that little slip of paper, I could take a little fellow, who could scarcely walk across the room because of damaged heart valves, to the Army hospital. There he could get the best medical and surgical care available in Vietnam, including a "valve job," for free.

The Army hospital was well-staffed, with specialists in all the major areas. These doctors were drafted, and usually stayed for about eleven months. At that time there was not a lot of military activity in the Saigon area itself, and so these doctors were sort of sitting there twiddling their thumbs. A fairly high percentage of them were not in favor of the war, and were not happy about being there. They knew that outside the military compound, on the streets of Saigon, were some very interesting and unusual cases of illness and disease that they had not seen before, and they were very eager to help.

To me as an MCC worker, however, the hospital represented a system which I opposed. Could I reject the basic reason that the hospital was in Vietnam, but then cash in on its presence because my Vietnamese patients needed the help? And with all the identity problems that I already thought I had, could I expect to relate to the Army Hospital in such an indebted way, and still keep my identity clear as a nonresistant Mennonite with MCC?

The pressure from the other side, of course, was that we had Vietnamese people who needed medical care. In many cases we could not provide the care, nor could it be provided by other hospitals in Saigon. Dr. Smith-T from our clinic was the connecting link that made this care even more available. Wisely, the Mennonite church in Vietnam and my Eastern Mennonite Board colleagues did not make this decision for me. They said they would support me either way.

I am not a person given to visions and dreams or their interpretation. But early one morning, after I had been thinking through this the night before, I suddenly found myself "over there." I had left earth, and I was talking to the Lord, reporting in. When I mentioned that I had spent these years in Vietnam, I hurried to assure God that I had really tried to keep my identity clear, that I had not become confused with the U.S. military or its mission. I will always remember the sadness of His eyes as together we looked down on earth, and saw my Vietnamese friends struggling with lives of difficulty. Some were not able to see, some were not able to walk, and others had various problems that could have responded well to treatment.

I will always remember the sadness in God's voice when he said, "But those are my children too." And suddenly my concern about keeping my hands clean and being sure people knew what I believed didn't matter anymore.

I have thanked God many times for the certainty and the assurance that experience gave me, not only for my life in Vietnam, but for the rest of my life as well.

We soon began to take patients into the Army Hospital every Tuesday afternoon, when they held clinic for Vietnamese patients. I'll always remember the shock I had one day when I brought a group of Vietnamese patients into the hospital. I was at the registration desk when a young American soldier looked at me, stood back and said, "You know, I believe you really like these gooks."

It had never occurred to me that he would think that I didn't like these patients that I had brought to the clinic. I said, "Yes, these are my friends, and I've had the opportunity to get acquainted with them under circumstances which are very different from yours."

One day one of the American doctors, a tall man in military fatigues, said to me, "Hey, who are you anyway? Who do you work for?"

I told him that I worked for Vietnam Christian Service, and that I was a Mennonite.

He said, "Mennonite, that sort of rings a bell, but I can't think who they are. What would be unique about you or your beliefs as Mennonite?"

"Well," I said as I stood there and looked up at this man in Army fatigues, "for starters, just between you and me, we could say that Mennonites don't believe that war is an answer to the problems that we face."

His face changed and he grinned, "There are some more of us that believe that too."

I told him that I had always felt a little apologetic about bringing in so many people for medical help. I shared my worries about what might happen if he and the other Army doctors really knew what I believed. I asked if he wondered how I could bring patients in to the hospital, given the beliefs I held.

During our conversation, he took a seat, but as I finished, he got up and started pacing back and forth in front of me. He said, "Don't you ever say that again. God knows that we're doing enough damage over here. And who are you to make decisions that would keep us from doing some good?"

I felt reassured. I'm sure that not all the doctors felt the same way, but certainly there were a lot that did. I think they shared his appreciation for the opportunity to do what they could to help the Vietnamese people.

As I think back over this experience in the light of my total pilgrimage, I can't help but smile at the irony of the whole thing. A little Mennonite MCC nurse was probably responsible for taking more Vietnamese patients into an American military hospital than any other nurse in Vietnam during that two-year period. I can't help but feel a little philosophical. I know that God leads us in very exciting and interesting ways. I just thank him for this experience, and for walking with me through it.

Sermons on the Street

Over the past twenty-five years, Joan Gerig's faith pilgrimage has included a growing commitment to public witness for peace and justice. Joan began as a somewhat reluctant participant in a peace march in Goshen, Indiana, in 1968, in the aftermath of Martin Luther King's assassination.

I was so shy," Joan recalls. "I wasn't against demonstrations, they just weren't in my orb. I remember though, as I arrived at the demonstration site, I walked behind a mother pulling her child in a wagon. This made the event seem like a safe place to be."

Since then, Joan has often used the sidewalk and the street as places to share her witness to peace, and her personal commitment to those who seek justice around the world. Whether organizing a vigil at the South African consulate, or standing in front of a tank during an armed forces parade, Joan credits the church for nurturing her faith and convictions.

"The church has given me all the experiences that have gone into this," Joan explains. "I was a Voluntary Service worker in a poor community in St. Louis; in Winnipeg I helped educate wealthy people about what corporations are doing in third world places; and I was an MCC worker in southern Africa for six years. The church has given me these experiences, and I've attempted to act on them." The church in South Africa inspired Joan to organize a witness against the injustice of apartheid in front of the South African consulate in Chicago. "The young people that were coming to Botswana, literally running from South Africa—Soweto—were so politicized. They didn't allow anyone to stand on the fence—one was either for apartheid or against it. They asked me, 'What are you going to do? How are you going to help us when you go back to North America?'"

In 1988, Joan received a letter from a South African Christian who told her about the "Standing for the Truth Campaign"—a grassroots effort to help churches find the courage to tell the truth about the injustices of apartheid. In an atmosphere of intimidation and violence, fear is a significant obstacle to overcome in the struggle for justice. Joan's friend wrote, "You have got to do something to help us!"

Joan prayed and discussed ideas with others. "I felt duty-bound to do something," she remembers. "I wanted to be faithful to the church members in South Africa." Out of this discernment process, she and others organized a silent vigil against apartheid at the South African consulate. The vigil lasted for six hours, but the silence was broken by enthusiastic high school students who sang songs.

"We couldn't stop them," remembers Joan. "I decided then that we would somehow have to make use of music in our vigils."

Out of this experience, Joan and others launched an annual "Sing Out Against Apartheid." For the past three years, Martin Luther King Day has provided the occasion for choirs and singing in front of the South African consulate. "Music is less threatening than chanting and banners," notes Joan. "We always take pictures and send the news articles back to our friends in South Africa, to help them know that we care about them."

While Joan has personal links to South Africa, she also felt drawn to join others in resisting the Contra war in Nicaragua. During the 1980s, the Reagan administration provided military assistance to Nicaraguan rebels who were trying to overthrow the Sandinista government. The guerrilla warfare which ensued killed an estimated fifty thousand people, including many civilians. Once again, Joan felt that she had to declare her commitment to peace and stand with the victims of war.

"We haven't paid federal income taxes for the past nine years," explains Joan. "We've been doing voluntary service, so that the money we do earn through our employment can more easily be shared with others and support life-giving causes. Even though it wasn't my money which went for the Contra war, I was part of a system which sent the money there, and allowed me to live a reasonably middle-class life. Realizing this, I wanted to be a part of the people who were trying to prevent the money from being sent."

This conviction led Joan to participate with other Christians in an act of civil disobedience. During a rally which voiced opposition to more military aid to the Contras, Joan and five others knelt to pray in the cubicles of a revolving door, blocking access to the

Federal Building in Chicago.

They were quickly removed from the door, and the entrance to the building was not blocked for a significant period of time. Yet the impact of this act is one which Joan still feels within her. "A new power has come to me. I do not feel powerless. I admit to being rather short with people who say there is nothing we can do. We can do something. Action gives us courage and wisdom to take another step.

"The most successful actions are the ones that express our faith in some way, like praying in the revolving doors. If you are explaining something to people, it has to come from your depth. My depth is in spirituality, not political analysis."

Much of Joan's support for applying faith to issues of peace and justice in the public arena comes from the faith-based community of which she is a member. "In our group, you do what you are ready to do. You're not pushed. At every meeting we have some prayer and meditation together. We build relationships. We don't just act as lone individuals. When we make a public witness, we do it with others. That's what we are—a community that eats together, shares together, and goes into action together. And we process it when it's over. That's something I think that the church hasn't taught us so well. After you've done an action, you have to stop and think about what was right, what was useful."

This kind of community support gave Joan the courage to stand in front of a tank at the annual armed forces parade. She and several others from her community decided to walk into the street in front of the armed forces parade in order to bring it to a halt. Joan remembers feeling a lot of fear as she waited for the right moment.

"The kids that I knew from South Africa had run in fear from tanks like those in the parade. Other people talked about tanks like these in the Philippines. I thought of these experiences when I saw the tanks coming down the street.

"I was scared. I was terribly frightened. But I knew I wanted to take this action. I had made promises to others, so I was sure that I would go through with it."

When the time came, Joan joined others in walking toward the middle of the street to stop the tanks. Plainclothes police came quickly, however, and arrested Joan before she could stop the parade.

"In the police station, some of the police wanted to let us go right away and others didn't. There was a lot of bantering and some serious talk. Humor is very important. It helps people drop their facades. I always try to humor the police. If we are singing, I share my music with them and ask them to sing along. Sometimes I get my picture taken with the police."

Joan likens her acts of civil disobedience to a sermon. "Our interest is always in communicating. We try very hard to do our best. This is our sermon. It is our chance to witness to literally millions of people if there are TV cameras around. We want to make our statements in interesting and gripping ways.

One of Joan's concerns about civil disobedience is its impact on her daughter's sense of security. "Orlando and I take turns doing civil disobedience. We have told Tasara that we would never both be in jail at the same time. In the beginning, she got very concerned. The first time Orlando went to jail, she was five years old, and had just heard the Sunday school story about Steven being stoned and Paul being put in jail. When I told her that her dad was in jail, she thought he was going to be stoned and she was very scared. Once she understood that people weren't going to throw stones at him, she was all right.

As Joan reflects on the meaning of her sermons on the street, she recalls an experience which happened a number of years ago. "I was called to testify on behalf of a friend who had been arrested for civil disobedience. The prosecuting attorney who cross-examined me tried to discredit me as a witness—he kept asking how many demonstrations I had already participated in or helped to organize.

"I remember that I quizzed him a bit about his definition of a demonstration. He continued the same line of questioning, however, so I finally said, 'Sir, I hope my whole life is a demonstration!'

"That's still the way I feel," says Joan. "The actions I take on the street are no different from the choices I make about where I live and worship, or where I buy my groceries. These choices, like my sermons on the street, reflect who I am and what I believe about the world and the church."[1]

How Eve Yoder
Triumphed in Defeat

During the turbulent days of the American Revolution, Patriot leaders and the new Continental Congress often used a loyalty oath as a means of sorting out friend and foe. The Pennsylvania General Assembly passed such a loyalty test on June 13, 1777. All white men, eighteen and older, were required to pledge their loyalty to the free and independent state of Pennsylvania and to renounce the king of Great Britain. Penalties for refusal to take the oath included retraction of the privileges to vote, hold public office, do jury duty, sue for debts, or transfer real estate by deed.

Mennonites and Quakers refused to affirm their allegiance, troubled by the gap between unqualified allegiance to the budding nation and their biblical understanding of being subject to the ruling authorities. The oath would cause them, against their consciences, to take sides in a war.

When Sir William Howe invaded Maryland and Pennsylvania in the summer of 1777, hostility to British sympathizers and neutral citizens grew. In December of that year, Maryland passed the "Act for the Better Security of the Government." Under this new ruling, all who failed to take the loyalty oath were subject to tripled county and state taxes, and were barred from practicing the professions of medicine, law and education, and were not allowed to preach or teach the gospel. Other states followed suit. Pennsylvania also added harsh new penalties and a deadline of June 1, 1778 to its earlier test act.

The following story, by historian Richard MacMaster, relates how one woman responded when her husband was banished and their personal property confiscated because he refused to take this oath of allegiance.

A country auction always draws a crowd. Long before Sheriff

John Siegfried arrived to begin the sale, neighbors, bargain-hunters and sympathetic relatives milled about the Yoder farmyard, looking over the furniture set out on the grass, trying to guess the prices the cattle and horses would bring. Bidding would not run very high, for hard cash was a rare commodity in eastern Pennsylvania in 1778 and Jacob Yoder's place would be the eighth Mennonite farm sold out in Northampton County in as many days.

People kept coming. They crowded around the front steps to hear the sheriff solemnly proclaim that on this first day of September in the second year of American independence all the property of Jacob Yoder of Upper Saucon Township would be sold at absolute auction. He repeated his announcement in German, then stepped down and a professional auctioneer began coaxing bids out of the crowd.

Eve Yoder watched the proceedings dry-eyed. They began with hogsheads, barrels and grain in the barn, things of no great value and of no special meaning to the family. The auctioneer had her spinning wheel now. How many winter evenings had she worked at it? It went for a few shillings. The auctioneer and the crowd moved on. The walnut table. Sold. The sheriff himself bought the chair and stools from the kitchen!

So it went all morning. The household furniture was soon gone. Before the crowd drifted out to the barn to bid on their livestock, the sheriff's men brought out the big five-plate iron stoves that heated the house. They had unbolted them, pried them loose, and dragged them out, pipes and all. Jacob Bachman told the sheriff they were part of the house, but he paid no attention. The stoves attracted some competitive bidding and went for a good price. The crowd moved away from the house, anxious to bid on Jacob Yoder's horses, his two wagons, his cattle and sheep, the plows and harrow, the cradle and scythe.

When the last wagon drove away from the farm, laden with tools and furniture and bags of flaxseed, a cow tethered behind, Eve Yoder and her children were left with the farm buildings, the soil, and some standing grain. The sale brought seven hundred pounds, a fraction of what it was worth, for Jacob Yoder had been one of the best and wealthiest farmers in Northampton County. Eve Yoder would not get a penny from the sale. Everything her husband owned was confiscated by the Commonwealth of Pennsylvania. The law allowed their oldest boy to inherit the farm itself, as if his father were dead.

Jacob Yoder was not dead. He was in jail in Easton, along with nine other Mennonite farmers from Upper Saucon Township. In the last days of August 1778, Sheriff Siegfried had sold each man's property. They had thirty days to leave Pennsylvania, never to return, on pain of death.

What crime had they committed? Each one had paid his taxes and minded his own business, keeping away from politics. As nonresistant Christians, none of them could fight in the army, but several of them had allowed their wagons and teams to be requisitioned to carry food to Washington's army and bring back wounded men. They were not dangerous enemies to be banished from the state.

Earlier that summer, Frederick Limbach, a neighboring farmer and justice of the peace in Upper Saucon Township, had issued warrants for every Mennonite in the township. Limbach had visited each one in turn and they had all refused to take an oath of allegiance to the state. He had them summoned to Easton. When they refused the oath a second time in open court, the judge banished them and confiscated all their property.

The peaceful people could not pledge their allegiance, for the same reason they could not fight. "It is against my conscience," one man told Justice Limbach, "because we shall be at peace with everybody and forgive all men." Another Mennonite called it "an oath of enmity." They would gladly promise "to be true to the state according to the doctrine of St. Paul, Romans 13, be subject to the higher powers, but as a defenseless people, we could have nothing to do with setting up or tearing down governments."

They were willing to pay the penalty imposed by the law, to be subject in this way to their rulers. Many people who refused the oath ignored Justice Limbach's summons. But the Mennonites all made the long trip to Easton, knowing they would go to jail and lose everything they had.

Eve Yoder could not read the law that condemned her husband or follow the arguments of the lawyers in Easton court, but she knew when an injustice was done. Mennonites, Quakers, Brethren, and Moravians had all refused the oath. Did the law intend to drive all these decent people out of Pennsylvania and rob them of everything they owned? William Penn made liberty of conscience the glory of his colony; did this new government mean to take it away?

Jacob Bachman tried to save his father's property by appealing to the Pennsylvania Assembly, but it did no good. Dr. Felix Lynn and other neighbors had signed petitions, but they were ignored. Some Philadelphia Quakers went to see the French ambassador to ask his help in getting the sentence on the Upper Saucon Mennonites changed, but he refused.

Eve Yoder was sure that if the men in the Assembly knew how they were suffering, they might do something about it. With winter coming on, these Mennonite families had only what food neighbors could spare. They had no way of heating their houses. Abraham Geisinger's wife was in her eighth month of pregnancy without a single bed in the house for herself and her children.

Esther Bachman, George Bachman's wife, agreed to join her in telling their story. They found someone to put it down in English and someone to take it to Philadelphia.

The Assembly was meeting for the last time in that session, when their petition arrived. Members had their bags packed and were anxious to get home. But they found Eve Yoder's petition so shocking that they ordered an immediate investigation. They asked the state treasurer to make money available to at least partly right the wrong. When they met again in December 1778, they repealed the law, releasing Mennonites and Quakers from every county jail in Pennsylvania. In the meantime, Justice Limbach had been busy offering the oath to all the Moravians in Bethlehem, Nazareth, and Emmaus. Before he had gone very far, he received an order from Philadelphia to stop harrying innocent people. Eve Yoder and Esther Bachman had helped win religious liberty for all the people of Pennsylvania, not by fighting battles or making eloquent speeches, but by the only Christian way of responding to injustice, the way of suffering.[1]

In a Peace Tradition

M y grandfather who reared me was a chief," says Lawrence Hart of Clinton, Oklahoma. "Prior to his death in 1958 he made it known that I would succeed him. My extended family and the other chiefs approved.

"After his passing, preparations were made for me to become a chief. I went through the traditional ceremony. I had also gone through some instruction and found out there was a Cheyenne peace tradition."

Hart has researched the Cheyenne chiefs who were known as "peace chiefs." The foremost of these were White Antelope, Lean Bear, and Black Kettle. All three died violent deaths while holding to their peace positions. Many of the peace chiefs lived between 1850 to 1870, a time of severe conflict between Native Americans and United States military troops.

"If I have any role models it would be these, not only my grandfather, but those I read about," Hart says. "In the past few years we've developed a text called The Cheyenne Way of Peace. What has until now been oral tradition will be published."

Hart gives a great deal of credit for his basic outlook on life to his grandfather. His mother was not well after his birth and so he lived with his paternal grandparents. He was the sixth child in his family.

"My grandparents molded me," he says. "I was thoroughly Cheyenne until it was time for me to start school. I went to school my first year without knowing English. I was retained in the first grade because of that. Once I learned English, school was okay."

Another subtle influence was the pastor at what is now the Bethel Mennonite Church in Hammon, Oklahoma who taught the Mennonite peace position and encouraged Hart to attend Bethel College in North Newton, Kansas. Hart started there in 1952.

When he began college, Hart's goals were focused in the direction of the military. "Military service was a functional substitute for some of the male societies in the past," Hart says. He was ambitious to

Became first native American

excel in that area.

During Hart's second year at Bethel (Kansas) College, he came to know Larry Kaufman. They shared their futures with each other.

"His was completely different from mine," Hart says. "He was excited about going into PAX. That was a new form of service for the church then. PAX had just been developed by Mennonite Central Committee, as a form of alternative service in which young men could work overseas to help alleviate the suffering caused by modern warfare.

"I guess what really strikes me as I look back is that in spite of our diverse ambitions Larry was still a friend. He would talk to me about what he was going to do. He never did shut me off because my views were different."

Hart went into the military as planned, and Kaufman into PAX. They did not correspond with each other. In eighteen months Hart reached the goal he had set—he became a pilot in the Marines.

During the close of the Korean War in 1955 and in the advanced stage of Hart's training, some aces who had been pilots in the war were assigned to teach his group. They showed actual film footage of how they had become aces. The film depicted the shootings of planes and their pilots.

Instead of being impressed, many in the group were shocked at the killings.

Some began to raise questions about what they would be doing, Hart among them. He had maintained contact with the Mennonite church and its activities, and it affected him. And at that crucial point he learned that Larry Kaufman had lost his life by drowning in a river in the Congo (now Zaire). That's when he seriously asked himself who he was.

"When other fellows made decisions not to stay in the service, I did too," Hart says. "Whatever had motivated Larry was something I wanted. When my term was up I got out."

Hart decided he wanted to go into the pastoral ministry and went back to Bethel, and on to the Associated Mennonite Biblical Seminaries in Elkhart, Indiana. Then the Koinonia Mennonite Church in Clinton, Oklahoma, asked him to serve as their pastor.

Since that time, Hart has served the church and the Cheyenne people in various ways. Currently, he is Director of Community Services for the Cheyenne Cultural Center, Inc. He also serves on the board of Mennonite Central Committee, U.S., the Board of Trustees of the Cook Theological School, and is chair of the Council of Native American Ministries, Prophetic Justice Unit of the National Council of Churches of Christ.

Hart continues to be deeply committed to peace and to retaining the heritage left by the Cheyenne peace chiefs.

"I am convinced that many of the traditions of our people and their view of life are compatible with Christ's teachings. Not every church accepts Christ's teaching on peace. But the peace position makes me that much stronger as a Christian.

"I see many of our youth today who look at the church in general and who reject it because many of them say you can't be a traditional Cheyenne and a Christian. They need to have some of the same experiences I had. They need to look at some of the contemporaries of my grandfather to see how they can be Christian and Cheyenne."[1]

The Spirit of Melchizedek on Dürerstreet

Dr. Henk B. Kossen, former professor at the Mennonite Seminary in Amsterdam and at the University of Amsterdam, The Netherlands, shares his story about the question of paying military taxes.

I s it possible for people, who are seriously engaged in working for peace, to pay military taxes? In The Netherlands, the military portion is about nine percent of total taxes.

In the late seventies, when a movement began in The Netherlands to resist the paying of military taxes, my wife Elzelien and I got involved. We started by withholding 572 cents (about U.S. $2.80), according to a model proposed by the Defense-Tax-Refusal-Movement. This amount had a symbolic meaning, corresponding to the 572 NATO nuclear missiles which were placed in Western Europe.

Five hundred seventy-two cents was a very small amount. But withholding it meant an act of civil disobedience. Elzelien and I had never before done such a thing. This act did not mean that we wanted to deny the significance of taxes. We knew that a society cannot be run without taxes. We knew this very well. Therefore we did not keep the 572 cents for ourselves, but paid it into the unofficial peace fund of the Defense-Tax-Refusal-Movement. We also announced to the fiscal authorities what we had done and why.

These first steps did not have any effect. The fiscal authorities seemed to ignore them. So we went on to withholding 572 dimes (about U.S. $28.00). But this also did not yield any response from the authorities.

Then came the year 1983 and the Assembly of the World Council of Churches in Vancouver, Canada. I was the official delegate of the Dutch Mennonite Brotherhood and Elzelien joined me. There we made very strong statements against the production, deployment and use of nuclear weapons.

When we had returned to The Netherlands and again had to pay our income taxes, we decided to withhold 572 guilders (about U.S. $280.00). This could no longer be ignored by the fiscal authorities. Instead of approaching us, however, they tried to collect the withheld amount from the Mennonite Church Administration who paid my salary.

This was an interesting new development because now my own church was compelled to think about this issue. A long discussion took place within the Mennonite Brotherhood Council. Every member had to give his or her opinion. They decided to write a letter to the government, protesting the fact that the fiscal authorities had approached them instead of me. At the same time, they pled for a legal regulation which would allow this kind of conscientious objection, and even offered the help of Mennonite lawyers to design such a regulation.

The following year we again withheld 572 guilders. This time the fiscal authorities decided to approach us. They announced a public auction of our property. As soon as we heard this, we started to mobilize people to assist us. The staff at the Defense-Tax-Refusal-Movement office convinced us of the importance of publicity and helped us prepare a program for the auction.

I also went to a former student of mine, who had become a reporter and was working at the General Dutch Press Agency. He put the news of the coming public auction on the telex to inform all the Dutch news agencies. The next morning reporters started to call us, and I had to give a number of interviews. Elzelien informed the Women for Peace organization in which she is involved. They provided us with banners and loudspeaker equipment.

In the meantime, the bailiff from the tax office had put an official announcement of the auction on our front door. I placed an explanation of our reasons next to it. This paper became something of an opinion board. Someone wrote on it, "My sympathy." Another wrote, "It's your own fault." This comment was then crossed out by a third person.

The day before the auction I wrote a letter to all of our neighbors to explain what would happen the next day and why, and to invite them to be present. We fastened a large banner on the outside of our house.

On the day of the auction, we were well prepared. We had to rise very early, because I had been invited by the local Amsterdam radio station for a breakfast interview about the auction.

When I came home, a lot of people were already making the necessary preparations, and the number of visitors was continually growing. We provided coffee for all. When our program started, there were more than one hundred people in our house and quite a lot outside in the street with several banners.

The staff person of the Defense-Tax-Refusal-Movement led the program, and invited me to be the first speaker. I bid all our visitors a cordial welcome, thanking them for their presence and assistance. I also explained that all this had happened because of our convictions which grew out of membership in an historic peace church.

Other speakers followed, including four members of Parliament and the chair of the Dutch National Council of Churches. Another speaker was a reformed pastor representing a new movement called Pastors against Nuclear Weapons. They had decided to use our public auction to present themselves publicly.

When the bailiff arrived, he could scarcely find a way through the multitude of people. He first read a brief ruling, which said that anyone could bid on the seized household articles and that they must be paid for in Dutch currency. For safety's sake, a government bidder accompanied him, to get the auction going. Each time he made a bid, the staff person for the Defense-Tax-Refusal-Movement would bid a dime more. Thus, a number of things, such as a table, a piano, a desk and a television set were bought by the Movement with our own money. In the end, no piece of furniture left our house. When the auction was over, the bailiff auctioneer was rewarded with a hearty "Long live the bailiff!"

After the auction, bread and wine were distributed among those present. In this way we referred to Genesis 14, where the Bible first deals with world politics and war. Melchizedek, the priest of the God of Highest Heaven, brought bread and wine to Abram, after he had defeated the world powers with a handful of men. (The next day one of our Dutch national papers had an article with the headline "Spirit of Melchizedek in Dürerstreet.") And so we reached the end of our program. Meanwhile, our house had been filled with flowers![1]

Investing in Peace

In 1988, Gay Brunt Miller was working for a small company of 130 employees owned by Johnson and Johnson in Horsham, Pennsylvania. Each year, J & J promoted two campaigns among its employees—The United Way and savings bonds. During the first year Gay's company participated in the savings bond drive, her superiors were very proud to report to corporate headquarters that they had one hundred percent participation (Gay was on a temporary payroll at that time and didn't count). Of all the J & J subsidiary companies, only two had the distinction of reporting one hundred percent participation.

Due to a promotion, Gay began working directly for the manager of the company, who also happened to be the chairman for the savings bond Drive. As preparations for the drive began, the manager became very eager to match the previous year's achievement. Gay decided that she needed to break the news to her boss that his own secretary may be the only employee who would not buy a bond.

As Gay talked about her position regarding savings bonds and the reasons she could not participate, the manager was obviously disappointed, and offered numerous counter arguments. Gay let the subject rest, but knew deep down that she still did not wish to participate in the bond drive. She discussed the subject with her husband and with her Sunday School class. After several weeks, she gave her boss the following letter.

Dear Jim,

Did you know that the money needed to adequately provide food, water, education, health, and shelter for the world's population has been estimated at $20.4 billion annually? The shocking reality is that the world spends nearly that much for armaments every two weeks.

In view of this kind of information and much more, I feel compelled to make a statement of my beliefs. I, as a person, as a Christian,

---

and as a Mennonite, feel I must be faithful to my beliefs that we are called to be peacemakers and to have no part in the insane buildup of arms and paying for war.

Rich (my husband) and I believe in working at peace. Certainly it is possible to find inconsistencies in our lives. Living a totally consistent life is very difficult if not impossible. But we try to be faithful where we can.

I have discussed the issue of savings bonds with my husband and approximately twenty persons at my church. I have been encouraged by them, as I felt myself, that this is one issue that is an issue of choice (not a legal issue), where I can be faithful. I feel I simply cannot participate in the savings bond campaign. Instead, I will be making a contribution to the Peace Section of Mennonite Central Committee in the amount of a savings bond.

This decision has not been easy as I do truly like working for you and want to do what I can to make you successful. I have reached this decision, not out of obstinance, but out of conviction. Though you probably will not agree with me, I hope you can accept and respect my decision.

> Sincerely and respectfully,
> Gay Miller

Gay and her supervisor discussed her decision after he had read her letter. He continued to express disappointment that he could not report one hundred percent participation, but he also noted his respect for her integrity in standing up for what she believed.

Just before the end of the savings bond campaign, the company received a memo from Johnson & Johnson saying, "If any of your employees cannot participate for religious reasons, these individuals may be removed from your total audience figure."

In reference to this memo, Gay writes: "I am glad that my manager and I had worked through the issue prior to this notification. It made me stronger for rising to this issue; and he also gained a greater respect for me as a person, which has been an excellent foundation for our working relationship."

Recruited by the Contras

Mennonites in Honduras and Nicaragua were deeply affected by the violence of the Nicaraguan Sandinista and Counterrevolutionary (Contra) war of the 1980s. Just before Palm Sunday, March 23, 1986, the Sandinistas began heavy shelling and bombing on Contra positions near the small Honduran border town of Moriah. In subsequent troop movements on Palm Sunday, the Contras took over the Moriah Mennonite church building, using it to store arms and provide housing for their people. The Moriah congregation included both Honduran and Nicaraguan families, the Nicaraguans having come to Moriah in 1984 after leaving contested areas in their own country. Four of the Nicaraguan men from the congregation were recruited by the Contra forces.

While many of the Hondurans fled the fighting in the area, the Nicaraguans found it difficult to leave because they lacked the necessary legal papers. Eventually, many of the Nicaraguan families did flee to a refugee camp but not before the Contras had taken four of their young men: Jose Adan, Alfredo, Eliberto and Santos Ismael.

In the next weeks and months, these young men tried repeatedly to communicate their desire for release to family members and neighbors. One Honduran church leader reported, "I met one of the Mennonite youth when I was on the road. He was already carrying a gun and dressed as a soldier. Since he was with the Contras, he could not speak to me, but through gestures and tears he communicated to me that he was there totally against his will."

In late April, several of them were granted a two-day pass to be with their families before leaving with the troops for Nicaragua. The youth shared their extreme desire to not be forced to train for war, and asked their families and other Honduran Mennonite leaders to do whatever they could to press for their release.

In late May, Jose Adan showed up in Moriah extremely sick with tuberculosis. The Contras had left him behind when they went to the border. A Mennonite family still living in Moriah cared for him and tried to get permission for him to go to Danli (the next largest town) for medical treatment. Two months later, he was finally able to go. He then entered the nearby refugee camp where his wife had just given birth. Unfortunately, the child died of whooping cough in December.

Alfredo was able to obtain a four-day leave at the end of May to see how his father's crops were progressing. While in Moriah, he begged two Mennonite men to help him escape over the mountains since he did not know the way himself. Fearing for their lives, both men declined. They knew that if they were going to be able to stay and farm their land in Moriah, they could not help young men escape from the Contras.

In desperation, fifteen-year-old Alfredo deserted the Contras in early June. He was picked up by the Honduran military, however, and everyone assumed he had been returned to the Contras and killed. His friends were surprised when he showed up in Danli nine months later. Apparently, the military had allowed him to stay in a nearby province, and he had had no way to contact his family members who were now in the refugee camp. When he applied for legal papers to stay in Danli, Honduran immigration officials deported him to Nicaragua. Amazingly, Alfredo returned to Danli once again, making several bus trips through Honduras without any money or official papers. This time he was able to obtain permission to stay in Danli near his family.

After numerous appeals from Honduran and North American church leaders, Santos Ismael and Eliberto were finally released in late 1987, eighteen months after being picked up. Promised good-paying civilian jobs with the Contra forces, both thought at first that they might return to the base after visiting family members. Renewed contact with family members and the church, however, persuaded both Santos and Eliberto to stay with their families, despite the grinding poverty of the refugee camp.[1]

Staying True to God's Call

The Bruderhof community (Society of Brothers) had its beginning in 1920 under the leadership of Eberhard Arnold. A decade later, the Bruderhof communities united with the Hutterian Brethren, a nonresistant Christian community with roots in the sixteenth century.

Born in the aftermath of World War I, the pacifist convictions of the Bruderhof community went deep. As Hans Meier, one of the Bruderhof leaders explained, "Many Christians felt that the war was a call to repentance, a call to change their lives from an empty and hypocritical confession for Jesus to a real following of Christ in love to one's neighbor and to one's enemy."

Hans was deeply affected by the war. A native of Zurich, Switzerland, he recalls, "My father was a Socialist and member of the Trade Unions. I remember him telling me that there would be 'no more war' because the workers of all the countries had sworn to strike if their governments should declare war. When I asked why there was a war going on in the Balkans, he pointed out that the people and workers there were not so well educated and organized as they were in Switzerland, Germany, Austria, France, Italy, and England. I was therefore deeply shocked in 1914 when the majority of all those 'well educated' Socialists enthusiastically went to war. Switzerland was surrounded by the warring nations. Although politically neutral, Switzerland made ammunition for both sides. Through Switzerland, the Red Cross exchanged prisoners of war who were so crippled that they were unable to fight anymore. He could observe hospital trains full of thousands of young men without legs or arms, or blind, or with mutilated faces and bodies, returning to their home countries on both sides. The main churches on both sides blessed the soldiers and their weapons in the name of God and Christ. The real victory in the war was on the side of the powers of death and misery for millions of human beings."

Hans became "an ardent pacifist." He and his wife, Margrit,

poured their energies into peace work and attempted to live in community with others. Eventually, their faith journey brought them to the Bruderhof community in the Rhön area of Germany. Arriving just before the outbreak of World War II, they were unaware of how their pacifist convictions would be tested again and again in the years ahead.

"Margrit and I and our little son arrived at the Bruderhof on the very day that Hitler came to power. Eberhard Arnold, who had a deep understanding of the historical atmosphere and situation of the hour, knew immediately what this change in the government meant for Germany and the world and for the community. In many letters to the government and even personally to Hitler, Eberhard expressed the united determination of the Brotherhood to stand for and represent only the Gospel and the discipleship of Jesus Christ, at the same time asking God to protect the government so that they could truly fulfill the task God had given them, warning them earnestly not to shed innocent blood. Eberhard warned all the members of the Bruderhof either to be ready for persecution or else to leave. A few guests and novices left the Bruderhof, and the rest of the members united in faith for the task of giving a living witness for God's Kingdom, in contrast to all the kingdoms of this world.

"With this attitude we could never use the enforced public greeting of 'Heil Hitler' (which would have meant that we expected salvation from Hitler), and when officials insisted on this greeting, we answered that we wished everybody the best, including Hitler, but that we expected salvation only from Christ.

"The first official reaction came after the plebiscite in November, 1933. On the ballot-paper was the question whether we agreed with the politics of Hitler. We answered with personal signatures that we stood only to the way of the Gospel of Jesus Christ with our whole life and that we asked God that His will be done also through the men of the government. A few days later over one hundred of Hitler's soldiers led by a Gestapo (secret police) chief, revolvers ready in their hands, stormed the Bruderhof from all sides and started a thorough search for hidden weapons.

"They were very disappointed not to find any trace of violent opposition to the State. The result of this visit was an order from the police that closed our school and forbade us to take any visitors in. 'It is all right,' one of the officers told us at the end of their visit, 'if you preach to one another, but we will not let you make any propaganda for your faith, and your children will be educated by teachers who conform to the new time in Germany.'

"In the next few days we sent our children of school age and German nationality to Switzerland and, after a month there, to Liechtenstein, since the Swiss Government would not allow them to stay in their country out of fear of Hitler.

"We invited the seriously seeking visitors to be members of our household and warned the superficial ones of the danger of being persecuted with us when living with us—this made them soon leave.

"The government forbade us to sell our books. After repeated applications for permits to sell our books, we received an answer from the chief of police that throws a light on the whole situation until our dissolution:

'My rejection of a permission is based not on the personal unreliability or unsuitability of these persons but exclusively on the fact that the propaganda that emanates from the Bruderhof is dangerous to the State. They repudiate the priority of the interests of the nation and the State, even as they refuse to recognize the basic national socialistic laws about blood and race.'

The chief of police also referred to the fact that the Bruderhof community opposed military service, sending their young men of military age to Liechtenstein to avoid military duty.

In spring of 1936, Hitler's government requested the forced extradition of the Bruderhof young men in Liechtenstein. A tiny and powerless country, Liechtenstein informed the Bruderhof that it would need to find a new place for its young men.

The Bruderhof sent some English members (who had joined the year before) to scout possibilities in England. In the meantime, France closed its doors to all Germans, leaving the Liechtenstein group virtually trapped.

"Three brothers were in greatest danger," writes Hans, "and one of them was not even allowed to enter Switzerland. We decided that the three brothers would have to go via Italy, the only country without entry restrictions for Germans, and from there find any possible way to England. I was asked to accompany them. The steward emptied his cash box to the last cent and gave me the equivalent of thirty dollars."

After numerous difficulties, including hunger, interrogation and a night's journey through the tense French/Italian border area, Hans and his three companions arrived in England, just in time to celebrate the opening of the Cotswold Bruderhof in Wiltshire.

Hans then returned to Germany, where, "in 1937, the German

government used the Gestapo to confiscate the Rhön Bruderhof. They asked us to pay our debts, after they had confiscated everything we had!"

The Gestapo took the Bruderhof's executive committee into "protective custody." This committee included Hannes Boller, Karl Keiderling and Hans Meier (Eberhard Arnold had died suddenly in 1935). The other Bruderhof members were allowed to leave. Fortunately, they were taken in and cared for by Dutch Mennonites in a very loving way until they were able to emigrate to England.

Meanwhile, Hans and his two companions spent their time in prison reading the Gospels and Gottfried Arnold's History of the Churches and the Heretics. They were eventually released from prison by a sympathetic judge and were able to follow the other Bruderhof members to the Cotswold Bruderhof in Wiltshire, England, despite much danger and the fact that none of them had valid passports.

Hans continues, "Although the communities were situated in Wiltshire, which was very conservative, our neighbors were in general very friendly toward the community until after the defeat of the British and French forces and their evacuation from Dunkirk in May 1940. Then everybody expected the invasion of the British Isles by Hitler's armies.

"Not unlike the experience of the Japanese Americans on the West coast after Pearl Harbor, from this moment on we experienced the mass psychosis of fear and mistrust toward any foreigner. The situation was aggravated by the fact that the Germans on the Bruderhof lived together in peace with quite a number of English citizens, who as conscientious objectors refused to defend their country with arms and for this reason were despised as traitors. The sale of produce from our garden, dairy, poultry and bakery was stopped. There were some nasty incidents when brothers were harassed by the Home Guard during inspections of the place. Two brothers once were ambushed in the night on their way from one Bruderhof to the other and saved themselves only by hiding underneath a haystack in the fields. Big concrete blocks were put in our field to 'prevent German parachutists or gliders from landing.' When neighbors saw an accidental light in the direction of the Bruderhof during a blackout, we were accused of sending light signals to the German bombing airplanes. Neighbors who in earlier times had greeted us and even invited us for a cup of tea now withdrew and shut their doors when we passed.

"By the summer of 1940 the situation in England had become very tense. The government in London approached us, saying that they had their hands full with the defense of the island and were no longer able to defend us against the unreasonable attacks of our neighbors. So they suggested that either they intern our German members for their own safety or that we emigrate. We felt that splitting up the community, especially along national lines, would be against the witness to peace in the spirit of a brotherly Christian life, so we decided to look for a country that would accept us."

Finding such a country proved to be a difficult and laborious task. Visa applications to join the Hutterite communities in Canada and the United States were both denied. Finally, Orie Miller from the Mennonite Central Committee approached the Paraguayan embassy on behalf of the Bruderhof. They were assured that they would be welcome in Paraguay under the same law as previous Mennonite immigrants. Under pressure to leave England as soon as possible, the community prepared to go to Paraguay.[1]

From Alternate Service to International Business

I remember World War II as a child in grade school," recalls Luke Wenger. "Even though we lived in the quiet countryside of Lancaster County, Pennsylvania, the war didn't seem far away. I remember collecting milkweed pods so that the fibers could be woven into fabric. We had to return empty toothpaste tubes in order to purchase new toothpaste. There were also practice air raid sirens and blackouts.

"What really made an impression on me were the pictures of people in Europe who were suffering from hunger. I remember the gaunt faces. This, coupled with stories in the newspaper about the dangers of communism, and the impending war with Korea made me worried."

Luke's response to the crisis is amusing in retrospect, but at the time it was the serious response of an eleven-year-old boy to a perceived danger. "I used to eat as much as I could," remembers Luke. "I'd eat a normal helping and then ask for more. I often ate meat, potatoes and bread even after I was full. I had decided that I should fatten myself up so that I would be ready for the hunger and hardship which would surely come to us. I really had my father puzzled. He couldn't figure me out!"

Today, Luke is a retired businessman, surprised at the interesting twists and turns in his life. As a young man, he had always assumed that he would live his life as a farmer. Instead, he became skilled in the field of respiratory therapy, and founded a business which produced medical equipment. Even as war and peace shaped some of Luke's earliest memories, it was these issues which nudged him off the farm into unexplored territory.

Luke's journey began in 1959 when he decided to take a couple years off before settling down on the farm. "I decided to join the 1-W (alternate service) program," he recalls. "I wasn't drafted by the

---

military, so there really were no compelling reasons to enter such a program. It just seemed like the logical thing to do. Many of my friends had done it. At the time there was a surplus of farm products anyway, and I wanted to do something which would be of service to people. I figured I would just do it for two years, and then go back to farming."

Luke entered a world of hospitals, lectures and training in respiratory therapy. He also entered the world of the big city, and began to meet people whose experiences and viewpoints were very different from his own.

"In Lancaster County, conscientious objection to war seemed normal. But somehow it felt a little embarrassing in the city of Philadelphia. Some of my colleagues at the hospital were Korean War veterans. These men had placed their own lives at risk in service to their country. I remember Roger, because we talked a lot and became friends. Roger had been wounded in the war. He walked with a distinct limp and required weekly treatments on his knee.

"I enjoyed my friendship with Roger, but I always felt a little uncomfortable about my own choices when I was around him. I began to wish that I hadn't chosen a paying job. In a way, I had simply changed careers. I hadn't really given up anything or taken any risks for peace. I had just moved from the farm to the city. Roger had put his life on the line."

After three years, Luke returned home, but not to the farm as he had earlier assumed. Instead, he was employed at St. Joseph's Hospital in Lancaster City, and set up the first respiratory therapy department in the County. While there, Luke's tinkering inclinations set him thinking about how the technology for respiratory therapy might be improved.

In 1967, Luke opened his own manufacturing business. He began by producing equipment which could measure the amount of oxygen provided to a patient, for more accurate and fair billing. As the business expanded, the product line included calibration equipment, pressure/temperature sensors and flow sensing devices. At the time of Luke's retirement in 1988, his business employed 175 people.

Over the years, some of the medical equipment was marketed to veterans' hospitals and military field hospitals. "Even in a relatively small company such as ours, it wasn't possible to be on top of all the details related to the company's operations. Some of our products were marketed to veterans' hospitals before I even knew about it."

In fact, as the years went by, the business supplied hospital equipment not only to veterans' hospitals, but also to the Armed Services which prepared back-up or emergency field hospitals for deployment in a time of crisis.

For Luke, however, these relationships with the military did not constitute an ethical choice, or a dilemma for his faith. "Hospital equipment helps preserve life. Life-saving health care should be available to all, whether or not the patient's lifestyle, political viewpoints, or career choices agree with our own. I supported the Mennonite provision of garden tractors to North Vietnam during the Indochina War. Just as wounded soldiers need life-saving help, so a people devastated by war need food."

As Luke's career as Chief Executive Officer of the company drew to a close, however, he encountered an economically rewarding opportunity which his moral and ethical values found difficult to accept. His international marketing agent, through participation in trade fairs, had aroused the interest of Communist China's army in the company's products and services.

"The Chinese were interested in oxygen-producing equipment for their military trucks which delivered equipment and supplies to a high altitude missile base. Given the thin atmosphere en route, drivers often experienced headaches or drowsiness as they traveled the steep and winding mountain passes. We had the capability of designing equipment which could extract pure oxygen from the air. The Chinese wanted this equipment for the safety of their truck drivers. The contract would have included several million dollars' worth of equipment, as well as the transfer of technology so the Chinese could continue production on their own."

Luke and his wife Shirley chuckled as they related this part of the story. "We used to talk about it over supper, and wonder how in the world a Lancaster County Mennonite could be faced with this kind of an opportunity," said Shirley.

"On the face of it, it would have been a good source of income, and lots of fun to do," said Luke. "It appealed to our egos—we had something they wanted! But we never gave it serious consideration. The technology was obviously for military purposes, and that wasn't for us. Our answer would have been the same had it been the U.S. Army."

The greatest difficulty for Luke was not in rejecting the contract, but in informing his international marketing representative that the

---

deal could not be concluded. "Because the sale could not go through," noted Luke, "he lost a good commission. As it turns out though, our representative knew enough about us to expect our answer. He wasn't surprised."

I Know My Hands Are Clean

The following story, related by Pastor Kobangu Thomas from Zaire, was recorded by Mennonite missionary Levi Keidel in 1963.

I was living in Archie Graber's house on Kalonda Station when fighting broke out in our Baluba village. I knew my tribemates would come hunting for me to help them.

I had the hunting gun Mr. Driver had helped me buy before independence. Art Janz had left his small gun in this house, too. I took them upstairs and hid them in the attic.

My Baluba tribemates came to my house and asked me to help them fight. They wanted me badly, because I am taller and stronger than most of them, and I had an American gun.

I told them it was not my affair to fight against flesh and blood, but against principalities and the powers of darkness. They did not like this. I told them that I would not cause the blood of other people to drain onto the ground.

Then they said I must give them the big gun. They were very angry and insistent. I told them that I was their pastor and my work was to save souls of people. How could I have a part in destroying their bodies?

This made them very angry. They said some of our tribemates would die uselessly because I refused to fight and because I refused to let them to take my gun.

They said that when the fighting was finished Pastor Kaleta Emil and I should flee because they would come back and kill us. Pastor Kaleta felt in his heart like I did.

When the fighting was finished, we did not flee. No one came to kill us. We found that our word was much stronger. People had greater respect for us.

I travelled widely with the missionaries and preached to many tribes. They greeted me with joy and listened to me. I can go to any of our tribes without being afraid somebody wants to harm me. They respect me as a man of God.

This is not the case for Pastor James. When fighting broke out, the desires of his tribemates overwhelmed him, and he went with them to war. Now that it is over, they don't look up to him as one above them in the affairs of God. They count him the same as anybody else.

How can a Christian ever be strong again when he as had a part in draining the lifeblood of others onto the ground? When I kill somebody I take the place of God and say, "Today your life ends. Today your soul must enter eternity."

Afterward I can weep tears of sorrow before God, and he will forgive me. But how can my tears ever change the place that soul went to? I could never make recompense for my sin. I could never after be the same. I could never forget.

Today I have much joy going to villages everywhere to preach the Gospel and talk to people about their souls. I preach with much happiness and power, because I did not let them use my gun. I know my hands are clean of human blood.[1]

To Baghdad for Peace

In November 1990, Gerald Hudson went to Iraq on a peace mission organized by Christian Peacemaker Teams. "It really wasn't a difficult decision," Gerald remembers. "I probably decided to go within the first five minutes after I was invited. Of course, I processed the decision with others, but it seemed consistent with who I am and what I believe."

While Gerald was in Baghdad on this mission of peace, his brother was on standby, waiting for orders to join Operation Desert Shield, the U.S. military effort aimed against Iraqi troops in Kuwait. Had Gerald's life unfolded a little differently, he might well have viewed Iraq through the sights of a gun, rather than through the eyes of friendship and faith.

Gerald grew up in southern Mississippi, one of seven children in a family headed by his mother. All four of his brothers dropped out of high school and joined the military. "It was contextual," explains Gerald. "We were trapped by southern politics and difficult economics. It was the 1960s, and Mississippi was trying to integrate its schools. In the process, the black community lost control of many of its schools, and many black principals lost their positions. We suddenly found ourselves in white-controlled schools, which caused a lot of tension for us as students.

"It was a particularly difficult time for black males. A lot of the rules frustrated us, like not being allowed to wear our hair African style. It seemed like every Friday there would be a riot of some kind. None of us thought we could make it. Out of 124 students who failed to graduate from high school during my senior year, 112 were black males."

In this kind of environment, Gerald's brothers and many of his friends saw the military as a possible solution. "My brothers didn't want to be a burden to my mother," remembers Gerald. "They wanted to be able to help support her. At least the military offered a job and a place to stay. We noticed that military veterans dressed better and seemed to have more money. Their cars were nicer. We looked up to them."

Despite this attraction to the benefits of military service, Gerald remembers another tug on his consciousness from an early age. "I grew up with 'churchianity,'" he says. "Every time the church doors were open, my family and I were there. My grandmother was a strong influence on us, and kept us involved in church. Jesus' teachings to love our enemies and our neighbors were ingrained in me. I didn't see the need to beat up on the white kids like some of my friends did. Some of the other black kids called me a 'honky lover.'"

By the time Gerald entered junior high school, some of the earlier difficulties related to integration had been smoothed over. Gerald had more choices, and began to believe that graduation was actually a possibility. He sensed that he could "succeed" without joining the military.

From his youth, Gerald admired Martin Luther King, Jr. Even though he didn't understand King's teachings on nonviolence, Gerald developed a desire to learn how nonviolence could work in the real world. Gerald's exposure to Mennonites deepened his growing conviction that violence was not the way of Jesus or the solution to problems.

After high school, Gerald enrolled at Eastern Mennonite College, where he met professors who reinforced his commitment to peace. He spent four months in Nicaragua and one month in South Africa as part of his studies.

Gerald's trip to Iraq was simply the next step in a journey of faith. "Each overseas experience had a deep impact on me," he notes. "I've learned that peace and justice cannot exist without each other. If peacemakers would speak and act with courage, injustice could be addressed before it turns into violence."

Despite Gerald's deep commitment to peace as a way of life, his relationships with his brothers in the military have remained open and strong. "Only recently has my one brother begun to talk about his experiences in Vietnam," says Gerald. "We recently went to the Vietnam Memorial together. That was a powerful experience for both of us.

"Another brother, a fifteen-year army veteran, was seriously considering military duty in the Persian Gulf. He advised me not to go to Baghdad because it was too risky. Before I went though, he called to let me know he supported me. When I returned from Iraq,

I urged him not to go to the Gulf with the army. Given his unit and his position, he had a choice about whether or not to go. In the end, he chose not to go.

"His choice not to go was a result of several factors, including his own critique of the military which had been developing over a period of several years. When I returned from Nicaragua in 1986, I sensed that we both had serious questions about whether or not it was right for the U.S. to try to police the world. Upon my return from Iraq, I shared my experiences with him, and raised concerns about the U.S. defense of Kuwait, a country without a democracy."

One of Gerald's strongest memories from his trip to the Middle East was a meeting with a young Jordanian reporter who had been a graduate of Georgetown University. "The Jordanian students are angry with the West," she told him. "They want Saddam Hussein to stand up against the U.S. Those who promote peace are criticized for not being faithful to the Arab cause. They are accused of not being real Arabs."

These words have stuck with Gerald. "We must strengthen the hands of those who promote peace," he says, "and witness against the dehumanization of people. Our lives have to be consistent with our words if they are to be credible. My trip to Iraq was an attempt to integrate my life and my words."

Refusing a Military 'Substitution' Tax

Bruno Sägesser is a member of the Mennonite congregation in Muttenz, Switzerland and a delegate on the Swiss Mennonite Peace Committee. Born in 1951, he is the father of seven children. Since 1989, he has reduced his workload at a chemical company to eighty percent in order to give more time to his family. He describes his experiences as a conscientious objector to military service and military taxes.

In 1971, I graduated from a seventeen-week military school for non-combatants in the army medical corps. As a follower of Jesus Christ, I felt pangs of conscience, and in 1972 I refused to take my first three-week refresher course. Since military service is obligatory in Switzerland and there are no alternative service provisions for conscientious objectors, I was tried by a military court. Fortunately, my heavy involvement with children and youth activities of the Blue Cross was recognized as proof of my sincerity. Nevertheless, I was imprisoned for three months, between a drug handler and a child murderer.

This was not the end of the matter. In Switzerland, all men between the ages of twenty and fifty who are not serving in the military must pay a "Military Service Substitution Tax." For several years after my prison term I did pay this tax. But this became increasingly difficult for me to do, so in 1983 I decided to refuse to pay this tax. Hopefully, I can continue this refusal until the year 2001, when I will be fifty years old.

For the first five years (1983-1988), the authorities simply contacted my employer, who then willingly paid my outstanding tax liability and deducted the amount from my wages. Then in 1989 and 1990, the highest court of Switzerland ruled that those refusing to pay the military service substitution tax must be imprisoned one to ten days each year. In my case, however, two lower courts refused to apply this penalty, and suggested instead a penalty of 150 Swiss Francs. As the first time when no prison sentence was required for this offence, my case attracted national press attention. It has also set a good precedent. At least one other person has also avoided prison, based on my case.

In deciding this question, I have been quite alone. My conscience clearly told me: what I cannot support with my body and spirit, I may not support with my money. My wife has fully supported me in this. Several of my co-workers on the Swiss Mennonite Peace Committee also support me, even though they are not yet ready to take the same step.

In 1984, I purchased the book, What Belongs to Caesar?[1] by Wolfgang Kraus at the Mennonite World Conference in Strasbourg. There I was encouraged to discover that people in Germany and North America also struggle with this matter.

In my own Mennonite congregation, I have not found the courage or the right occasion to talk about my actions. Both in my local congregation and in the Swiss Mennonite conference, past questions about peace have often led to dissent. Only after four years did I inform my pastor. I was encouraged to learn that he respected my decision. But I have been discouraged to hear people say that I have no chance for success because I am alone. My experience shows, however, that we Christians, with the help of almighty God, can accomplish things which appear impossible.

The way is still long. Currently, I live with the threat that the authorities will seize the tax through my wages. But the Lord has helped me so far and will help further.

I am concerned that I not be sentenced in a court where I have no opportunity to appear and give testimony. Rather, I hope that there can be open negotiations to which friends can accompany me. Then there is the opportunity to build relationships with the judges and it becomes more difficult for them to sentence according to a prescribed model.

There is also the urgent task of creating a truly civil alternate service option in Switzerland. The Swiss Mennonite Peace Committee has discussed this for years. Among other things, we suggest that once the conscientious objector to military service has served a prison sentence or alternate service assignment, he should be freed from payment of the military service substitution tax.[2]

Pressure on the Home Front

During World War I, the United States Congress passed an Espionage Law which made it illegal for anyone to discourage participation in the war effort. This law was used in several cases against Mennonite and Amish leaders who exhorted their people not to buy war bonds.

R
W. Benner and L. J. Heatwole, two Mennonite leaders, were tried and convicted under the Espionage Law. Senator George N. Conrad of Virginia acted as counsel for their defense and later described the situation:

"Last June, in 1918, some members in the Mennonite Church in Job, West Virginia, were informed that every person was to buy war saving stamps, or give his reason for not doing so. Some members applied to Reverend R. W. Benner, the preacher in charge of the congregation, for information as to what they should do, and he wrote to Bishop L. J. Heatwole for advice as to what attitude the members should take in reference to the matter.

"Bishop Heatwole replied that the General Conference of the Church had advised that they should contribute nothing to a fund that was to be used to run the war machine and he would give the same advice to the brethren in West Virginia. After receiving that letter, Reverend Benner wrote to a number of members at and near Job, advising them to go and give their reasons, but not to buy stamps.

"Agents of the government obtained one or more of the letters which Reverend Benner had written, and also obtained the letter which Bishop Heatwole wrote, and the grand jury of the United States court at Martinsburg brought an indictment against both Reverend Benner and Bishop Heatwole, charging that by their letters they had violated the Espionage Law.

"A plea of guilty was therefore entered and a fine of one thousand dollars each with costs was placed upon Bishop Heatwole and Reverend Benner respectively. It was considered by representatives of the government that these fines should be imposed, not so much as a punishment to Bishop Heatwole and Reverend Benner, but as a precedent and a warning to all other persons belonging to the Mennonite Church, or persons holding similar doctrines."[1]

Two other leaders who were indicted under this law were Manasses E. Bontrager, an Old Order Amish Bishop from Dodge City, Kansas, and Samuel H. Miller, the editor of *The Weekly Budget*, an unofficial Amish/Mennonite newspaper. Concerned about cooperation with the war effort, Bontrager wrote the following letter to The Weekly Budget:

Dodge City, Kans. April 24 - A greeting in our Saviors name.
People are all well excepting some colds.
The weather is cool again. Were having more rain than usual this spring.
Oats fields are nice and green much more barley is being put out this spring than usual on account of the wheat failing. A few farmers think they have some wheat that will be harvested, some corn is planted. As we are living in an age of time when the gospel is preached over a wider area than ever before, but in what state of affairs the world is in? A world war, never since the time of Julius Caesar was so large a portion of the civilized nations at war, never were such destructive weapons used to destroy life, never were the nonresistant people put to a more trying test in our country.
How are we meeting the great problems confronting us. Shall we weaken under the test or are we willing to put all our trust in our dear Savior? Are we willing to follow his foot steps? Our young brethren in camp were tested first, let us take a lesson of their faithfulness. They sought exemption on the ground that they belonged to a church which forbids its members the bearing of arms or participating in war in any form. Now we are asked to buy Liberty Bonds the form in which the government has to carry on the war. Sorry to learn that some of the Mennonites have yielded and bought the bonds. What would become of our nonresistant faith if our young brethren in camp would yield. From letters I received from brethren in camp I believe they would be willing to die for Jesus rather than betray Him. Let us profit by their example they have set

us so far, and pray that God may strengthen them in the future.[2]

Miller was away on church business when the letter arrived and it was his printer, A. A. Middaugh, who chose to print it on May 15, 1918, the twenty-eighth anniversary of the newspaper.   Several months later, Bontrager and Miller were both indicted under the Espionage Act and fined $500 each.   Miller was also fined $145.93 in court costs. Unable to pay the full amount, he spent several days in prison until his cousin, W. A. Miller, paid the fine.[3]

Peace and the Hardware Store

The typical hardware and appliance store in North America may have little occasion to talk to its customers about realities in the third world. The following letter shows how one hardware store attempted to fill a customer's order while introducing him to a third world craftsman trapped by poverty and armed conflict.

Lehman Hardware and Appliances, INC
4779 Kidron Road, P.O. Box 41
Kidron, OH 44636

Thank you for your order! Your business is important to us. Our goal is always to send every item from every order within 48 hours. However, the nature of our business (specializing in the hard-to-find) sometimes keeps us from doing this.

In spite of everything we've tried, we haven't been able to obtain any of the mallets you ordered.

Here's the problem: The especially dense and hard wood (called lignum vitea) used for them is only available in a few tropical areas. Ours came from Haiti. The fellow who makes the mallets lives on a river. His side of the river (fortunately for him) is controlled by the government. The other side of the river, where the wood grows, is controlled by the rebels (unfortunately for us). Naturally, he's not going to risk life and limb just to cut down a few trees. (See note below).

We have located another supplier. However, his mallets, which are virtually identical to ours, cost $6 more. Because of the vast difference in cost, we simply can't absorb it.

So I guess I'm presenting you with three choices: 1) Allow us to hold your order until our original supplier comes through. (We don't know when that will be.) 2) Pay $6 extra and receive the other mallet by return mail. 3) Cancel your order and receive a full refund.

I'm sorry we couldn't supply the mallet. Please contact us if you have any questions.

Thanks Again!
Galen Lehman

If you used Visa, Master Card, or Discover to place your order, you'll be glad to know we never charge your card until the merchandise has been shipped. (Returning this letter will simply let us know you want your back order torn up.)

Note: If not getting the mallet disrupts things for you, imagine what it does to the poor fellow who was trying to support his family by carving them. If you would like to help him and other Third world residents trapped by low-intensity wars, please send a donation to: Mennonite Central Committee (MCC), 21 S. 12th St., Akron, PA 17501. MCC sponsors mediation teams and relief efforts.

IMPORTANT: If you want us to cancel your back order, write your order number here (Order #   ) and return.

Thanksgiving Day in El Salvador

*Nancy Guthrie and her husband Gary were community develop-
ment workers with Mennonite Central Committee in El Salvador from
1987-1990.*

I t was one thirty in the afternoon on Thanksgiving Day 1989.
People all across the U.S. were settling down to a Thanksgiving meal with family and friends, thankful for the abundance
that God had given them.

I was thinking about that Thanksgiving Day spread when I was
suddenly jerked back to the reality of El Salvador as two A-37 jets
approached through the blue sky and flew over our home near the
Guazapa mountain. Helicopters hovered and circled nearby, ready
to go into action if needed. To my growing disbelief, the jets swooped
down close to town. I could see the bombs falling, they were so huge.
I had seen bombings before, but the location startled me this time.
Usually, the bombs fall on the mountain several kilometers away.
No civilians live there. These bombs were falling near the town of
Montepeque.

"The farmers must still be in their fields," I thought to myself.
"This is crazy! It is absolute madness!"

I went to the backyard, anxious to get a better view. I saw the
smoke billowing, indicating how close the bombs had landed. I
knew my friends were out there. I knew my government paid for the
bombs that fell there. I felt angry and utterly helpless.

Bombing and rocket fire filled the air for the rest of the afternoon.
I continued to wonder how my friends were, what they must be
thinking, feeling. But, as many times before, I was amazed at how
life in El Salvador goes on despite the noisy war so close at hand.
A neighbor boy had a birthday party that afternoon. The music and
games muffled the sounds of war, but didn't drown them out

completely.

The next morning the people of Montepeque came into town carrying their dead. Three people had been killed, including a father and son who were leaving their cornfield in an ox cart when a bomb hit them. The man's wife and daughter were seriously injured. The local military took them to the hospital for treatment, but offered no recompense for their terrible loss.

"Another man was cleaning beans in his field when the bombing began," a friend told us. "The helicopters were flying so low, they must have seen that he was carrying a stick for beating the beans—not a gun. But they killed him anyway."

What he said next made my stomach turn. "The helicopters flew low enough for us to see into them, to see the pilots. They weren't Salvadorans, nina," he said in a low voice. "They were 'rubios,' blondes, and had light skin."

I was limp with the realization that not only the bombs and the planes, but possibly even the pilots were made in the U.S.A. How can I communicate the unfairness of this crazy war to friends in the United States who just sat down to dinner on Thanksgiving Day?

I Love the Whole World

Anita Rhodes is a fourth grade student at the John Wayland Elementary School in Bridgewater, Virginia.

When I was in the second grade," says Anita, "I took a stand against saying the Pledge of Allegiance. My teacher said the Pledge of Allegiance every morning. I usually just stood or sat down, looking around. Sometimes I went out in the hall to the water fountain and got a drink. I didn't say it because I don't just love my country. I love the whole world."

"I remember the family had a discussion around the kitchen table about the United States," notes Anita's father, "and how it is really the homeland for the Native Americans. We talked about the American flag and how Native Americans might view it. I thought Anita grasped the concepts very well for a second-grader.

"I wrote Anita's teacher a note which gave my perspective as a parent about the Pledge of Allegiance. I said that because of our understanding of the Kingdom of God, it may be difficult for Anita to go through a quasi-worship experience by saying the Pledge of Allegiance.

"I wanted Anita to have the full range of options at school, from total compliance to a decision not to say the Pledge. I wanted it to be her decision. My note to the teacher was a way of helping her have the space she needed to make a choice."

Anita reports that she wasn't scared or worried about what the teacher or other children might say. Her fellow students asked her why she didn't say the Pledge. "I just told them that I love the whole world," she said.

At the end of the second grade, after she had refused to say the Pledge of Allegiance for a whole year, Anita was chosen by the faculty to receive the Good Citizenship Award.

Gunsmiths Who Quit Their Trade in Colonial America

The following story, related by Richard MacMaster, is set in the time of the American Revolutionary War.

John Newcomer was a gunsmith and a good one. The long Pennsylvania rifles he made in the shop beside his house in Hempfield Township in Lancaster County were accurate enough to pick off a deer nibbling on the far side of a cornfield or to win a ham or a side of bacon when men and boys gathered at a crossroads for target shooting.

Like other Pennsylvania gunsmiths, John Newcomer made every part and fitted the parts together himself. From the tip of the gleaming steel barrel to the polished wood of the stock, it was all his own work. When he engraved his name on it in capital letters, his rifle was signed with a sense of a job well done.

It took a strong man to handle one of John Newcomer's rifles. They were nearly six feet long with barrels more than four feet in length. But they were a great improvement over the cumbersome hunting guns that the English settlers used. It was little wonder that frontiersmen from Pennsylvania to the Carolinas prized the rifles made by the gunsmiths of Lancaster County.

The reputation of the Pennsylvania rifle, and the men who hunted with them on the Appalachian slopes, reached the Continental Congress of the United States. They called on Pennsylvania and Virginia to raise companies of riflemen and ordered the Lancaster County Committee of Observation to set those famous gunsmiths to work making rifles for the army.

John Newcomer made hunting rifles. His guns were advertised in the Philadelphia papers as "fowling pieces," guns for shooting ducks and rabbits, not men. If a pioneer took such a rifle off the pegs on the wall and fired it at an Indian passing too close to his cabin, John Newcomer had not made it to be used that way. Axes and shovels could kill a man in anger, too. But a rifle sold to the army had only one use.

On November 27, 1775, the Lancaster County Committee summoned John Newcomer to town to explain why he would not accept a contract to make guns for Washington's soldiers. He refused. He was fined and warned that he could not work as a gunsmith again. He would never again put his name on a rifle.

John Newcomer's family would not go hungry. He was a wheelwright and blacksmith and did some farming. It was not a great sacrifice. John Newcomer was an ordinary man trying to carry out in his daily business what Lancaster County Mennonites were saying in November 1775: "We find no freedom in giving, or doing, or assisting in any thing by which men's lives are destroyed or hurt."

His stand did not cost him the respect of his Hempfield Township neighbors. They elected him constable, which brought him to another difficult decision.

In July 1777, General Washington and his men waited anxiously for a new British offensive aimed at Philadelphia. Orders went out to call up the Pennsylvania militia.

Colonel Bertram Galbraith, a fighting Presbyterian from Donegal Township, was responsible for mustering the Lancaster County contingent. He sent word to the constable in each township to prepare a list of able-bodied men from eighteen to fifty-five years old.

John Newcomer refused to list the men in Hempfield eligible to be drafted into the militia. If he could not fight himself, how could he help draft other men? He was not alone in thinking that way. David Eshelman, the constable in Conestoga Township, Joseph Wenger, the Manor Township constable, and Abraham Whitmore, the constable in Lampeter, also declined.

Colonel Galbraith ordered them arrested and hurried them off to a Lancaster jail. At the August Sessions of the County Court, each was convicted and sentenced to pay a heavy fine.[1]

The Man Who Loved His Persecutor

Charles Cristano, a Mennonite leader from Indonesia, and former President of Mennonite World Conference, tells a story he remembers from a time of turmoil in Indonesia.

T here was a man whom I admired very much. He had a large family of seven children. He kept his home open to many, including strangers. He was not rich by some standards, but he made many people rich! The family lived among non-Christians. Though he and his family were ready to help, and generous in their own ways, they suffered persecution during times of war and racial tension. The first war was against the Dutch colonialists, and the second was against the Japanese occupation during World War II.

Since the family was Christian, many assumed they were collaborators with the Dutch who were also Christian, and traitors to the Indonesian people. Local people attacked the family's honor. The family suffered beatings and other humiliations. As a result, they had to seek sanctuary in a larger city as refugees. At one time the father was taken from the family by force, and they mourned him, thinking he was dead. They had no news for more than a week.

Their reunion was a mixture of great joy and great shock. With several cuts, cigarette burns and bruises, and a badly torn shirt and pants, the man showed the family what he had gone through. The great shock came when the man told his loved ones that the leader of his persecutors was a young man who had often had meals with the family. In fact, they considered him to be like a family member.

Several years passed. The whole family returned to their old home. One day a guest stopped to visit—the leader of the persecutors. The father received him kindly. Not only that, he invited the young man to stay for lunch.

Everybody was rather reserved at the table except the father. During their meal, the guest said nastily, "How did you survive the war? And how did you manage to start your business again? Did you receive money and crystal from your masters from the West?"

"No, our God cares for us!" the father said calmly.

After their guest left them, the children could not restrain their anger and disappointment. "Daddy, how could you forgive and tolerate such a man? You were nearly killed because of him!"

"To be honest I cannot forget what he did to us and to me, but our Lord tells us to love, even our enemies."

The man survived his enemies. He died at the ripe old age of eighty-four years. He was dear to many of us, close to our hearts. I have fond memories of him—he was my father.

Managing Military Contracts:

Conscience Against War in the Corporate World

C lifford Schott grew up in a Mennonite family in Ontario, Canada. As a youth, he was exposed to the issues of conscience related to peace during the second World War. His father's side of the family was not Mennonite, so some of his uncles joined the armed forces. His mother's side of the family was Mennonite, and all of these uncles declared themselves conscientious objectors to war.

While Clifford was too young to be confronted with a choice for or against military service during World War II, he embarked on an employment career which would offer him shades of that choice many times over.

Clifford took his first full-time job as a mechanical draftsman at age sixteen with Marsland Engineering Limited. This was a privately owned company, which began as a radio repair service, and expanded into radio and electronic component production. His first job was to draw and detail these components for record purposes and spare parts supply.

When Clifford took the job, he was not aware that during the war years Marsland's production of electronic components was almost one hundred percent military-related. With the war over, government agencies wanted all products documented in preparation for possible future needs.

Immediately following the war, the company grew very rapidly, moving into radio components, followed by television, along with ongoing supply of electronic components and equipment to the government. Marsland expanded into naval navigation and surveillance equipment which could be used for domestic navigational purposes, but was also suited for submarine or ship detection. At that time, Marsland did not produce parts for armaments.

According to Clifford, the President and owner of the company wished to become "the largest supplier of electronic components in Canada. He attempted to diversify and purchased new companies and products. He treated his employees well, and the employees responded with loyalty and support for whatever direction he wanted to go."

At this time, working on military contracts was not a critical issue for the twenty Mennonites working at Marsland. They rationalized, explains Clifford, "that the other products were life-saving rather than life destructive. While the church preached against direct military service, employment in industry was not questioned." One of Clifford's supervisors, a Mennonite, never expressed concern about military-related employment.

To be sure, they held firm convictions against taking human life. Yet, in the industrial world, it was not always easy to know what constituted a violation of this belief. "My profession was mechanical drafting, and was limited to the industrial environment. The possibility was always present for involvement to various degrees in supporting government activities. The only way out was to start over and change vocations. This then became a financial problem with a young growing family with financial obligations, based on an assumed level of income."

When war broke out in Vietnam, the American government ran short of mortar fuzes and experienced great difficulty getting sufficient American suppliers to meet their needs. The American government approached the Canadian government for suggestions of possible Canadian suppliers for these products. Marsland entered the bidding and won.

This did create both ethical and moral problems for Clifford and others. Clifford raised his concerns with his superior, but was not given any special consideration. All employees were expected to do the work assigned to them. To decline, even for religious reasons, could mean being relieved of employment.

The general manager expressed sympathy for Clifford's religious convictions, but stated that this was an opportunity to expand the business. He thanked Clifford and other employees for their good work and support in the past and strongly encouraged them to continue. Clifford was promoted to the position of Production Control Manager, with responsibilities for the scheduling and planning of all production, including that of the fuze.

"We talked as a group," says Clifford, "and decided we really did not have an alternative if we wished to continue using our strengths and expertise at reasonable salary and benefit levels. Moving to another company could have resulted in being in the same position again in a very short time. Amalgamations and sales of companies were happening every day.

"We decided to remain with Marsland and attempt to influence changes to non-military products. The potential for exerting a positive influence seemed stronger at Marsland due to management's respect for the Mennonite employees. It would have been difficult to build similar relationships at the same level in another company."

Clifford recalls a mood of resignation, and a strong feeling among many of the Mennonites that they didn't want to press the issue. "The majority of Mennonites were of Dutch and Russian background. They had experienced war and revolution, and had escaped with only the clothes on their backs. Marsland had provided them the opportunity to progress and provide for their families. They wished to enhance this relationship rather than place it in jeopardy. This created further problems for me in attempting to understand where they were coming from, as my family had not experienced the ordeals they went through to just remain alive. Why should I jeopardize their jobs?"

With considerable ambivalence, Clifford decided to continue his employment at Marsland. He notes that more encouragement and support from his church may have helped him make a different decision. His church did initiate a meeting with Clifford and another member who also worked at Marsland, asking them to discuss the status of their employment, and their decision about continuing.

For Clifford, the meeting was not helpful. "The meeting quickly became very one-sided, with criticism of our involvement, even after a lengthy explanation of our struggle and predicament."

Those who attended the meeting were primarily professional people, farmers, or self-employed business persons, who had attained good salary levels. Toward the end of the meeting, Clifford suggested that he would be willing to change employment if the church would be willing to supplement his salary and benefits until he could attain the level of his earnings at Marsland in another setting. There was little additional discussion, and Clifford had no further conversation about his dilemma with other church members.

Clifford doubts if he would have accepted financial assistance. Yet an offer of help would have expressed a sympathy and concern for his predicament which he desperately needed. In Clifford's mind, his problem was not entirely unique. "Without industry in the area, many of the people would not have employment and incomes at levels which they were experiencing." Clifford assumed that some of the food produced by the farmers was used to feed the army, and that some of the professors worked at universities whose research departments provided military support.

"These people were all at good earning or salary levels. They were quite eager to be critical of another brother, yet not willing to sacrifice themselves or accept a reduced standard of living. I believe that if any one of these brethren would have attempted to go beyond their own condemning actions and attempted to understand our predicament, I may have considered a change at the time, but their attitude determined my resolve to stay and it reinforced my feeling that this must be the right decision."

Clifford and another of the Mennonite Marsland employees, were asked to attend a meeting at the request of a church agency peace commission, to discuss the nature of their employment in light of Mennonite beliefs regarding war and peace. Clifford felt this meeting was similar to the meeting with his congregation. People asked questions, but did not offer solutions to his dilemma. In retrospect, however, he notes that "it may have been the meeting which pricked my conscience into looking at alternatives."

Other accounts of this meeting acknowledge the complexity of the issues, and lament the lack of support which Clifford received from the church. "Clifford is a kind and caring person, and obviously had already been struggling with this issue," noted one participant. "He did not get constructive help, and the church did not offer to back him up spiritually and possibly financially in a job change for conscience' sake."

Still, he was surprised that Clifford had attempted to justify his own high-level involvement in a company which produced war material. "His rationalizations were so obvious that I was almost speechless," he continued. "He was struggling with conflicting feelings as anyone raised in a Mennonite setting would be doing."

Initially, Clifford's decision to remain with the company appeared to be a good one. The company's owner decided to sell Marsland to Leigh Instruments Ltd., who purchased Marsland for its domestic products capability. Since Leigh's military products division was located in another city, this gave Clifford an opportunity to suggest that Marsland's weapons-related work be discontinued.

Clifford approached the new owners on moral and ethical grounds, as well as practical considerations. Clifford noted that he and other members of the management team were having increasing ethical problems with the fuze contract. He also suggested that military-related contracts were not very acceptable in a strong Mennonite community. At the same time, there were peace activists (Mennonites among them) who demonstrated against the company's military work. The combination of pressures from within and without led to some changes which pleased Clifford.

The fuze contract was discontinued. The management team worked hard to attract business for domestic products. New military-related contracts were taken by the other facility, thereby consolidating military and domestic production into separate facilities.

What appeared to be a happy resolution to Clifford's question of conscience, however, was not to last. Discontinuing the fuze contract, and competitive off-shore domestic products, led to a loss of profits. Layoffs became necessary, producing insecurity among the employees which remained. Over a two-year period, the number of employees dropped from thirteen hundred to seven hundred.

A newly-hired General Manager determined that fuzes and other weapons-related contracts could no longer be excluded from production. Clifford's old predicament had returned.

"This time I think the Lord spoke to me and did give me some direction. I was now at a senior management level—Production Manager responsible to the General Manager. I struggled and spent many sleepless nights.

"My eventual decision to leave Leigh was mainly due to my own discomfort with further involvement in armament production. I felt there was no further possibility of influencing the new General Manager who was determined to save the division at all costs, including the production of armaments."

At this time, the church Credit Union began to expand. A board member familiar with his problem urged Clifford to consider this kind of employment, indicating that the payment of competitive salaries was a problem. Clifford was attracted by the concepts of mutual aid and self-help, and found it gratifying to help persons in financial difficulty.

Clifford discussed his ethical struggles with the new General

Manager at Leigh, who was understanding of his dilemma. After consultations with his Head Office, the General Manager gave Clifford a generous gift in recognition of his many years of service with the company (Marsland and Leigh). This gift allowed Clifford to accept employment with the Credit Union at half salary for two years, when anticipated earnings would allow for more competitive salaries.

His struggles at Marsland, and the lack of empathy for his struggles from within the church, Clifford feels, helped prepare him for his later work in mutual aid.

"I had to experience how we have lost the practice of mutual aid and help for those in the church who are struggling. My experience and the experiences of others may encourage our young people to give consideration to peace and social concerns before they make vocational decisions and get themselves into uncomfortable situations. If we as Mennonites hope to make an impact on our own community as well as the community at large, we must demonstrate by example what we preach."

A Peaceful Dutch Warrior

Jan Gleijsteen, Sr. (1895-1989) lived in The Netherlands and was a member of the Singel Mennonite Church in Amsterdam.

At age nineteen, Jan Gleijsteen graduated with high honors with the degree of engineer to the merchant navy.

His career on the high seas was short-lived, however, for in 1916 he was summoned to serve in the Dutch army. Because of his excellent scholastic record, the army recognized his potential to become a high-ranking officer in the artillery division.

This was not in keeping with Gleijsteen's firm convictions on biblical nonresistance. A document from the military tribunal at Schoonhoven tells what happened next: "On the second of March 1916 Jan Gleijsteen willfully and repeatedly refused to be measured for a cap and other items of uniform, uttering, 'I refuse to serve in the military.'

Gleijsteen became the eighth Dutch conscientious objector since the draft was introduced in 1898 and the first Mennonite to refuse to serve in Holland's Landstorm (National Army).

Garrison commander Pannekoek, himself of Mennonite background, initially allowed Gleijsteen—in civilian clothes—to move about freely within the barrack grounds. But soon higher authorities placed him in solitary confinement in an empty cell.

By the time World War I was coming to an end—Holland maintaining its neutrality to the end—Gleijsteen was released with this note on his exit papers: "Because of his obstinacy Jan Gleijsteen has forfeited the privilege of serving in the armed forces for at least five years." This, of course, suited him just fine!

Unable to return to his chosen career because of his "criminal" record, Gleijsteen turned to nursing and eventually ended up working in a large mental hospital in the heart of Holland. There he met his future life companion, Gerritje Nowee, a nurse of French Huguenot and Lutheran background.

The Gleijsteens spent most of their married life as booksellers in Amsterdam. The Gleijsteen store was a technical, medical and Mennonite bookstore with a strong inventory of peace literature and a nice hoard of rare (mostly early Anabaptist-Mennonite) books and manuscripts.

In 1922 Gleijsteen, together with the pastors T.O. Helkema and Frits Kuiper, and laypersons such as Cor Inja, Gerard van Staden and others, founded the Workgroup of Mennonites and Quakers Against War and Military Conscription (renamed Mennonite Peace Group in 1946) to reintroduce the almost-forgotten principles of biblical nonresistance into the Dutch peoplehood.

Gleijsteen and Inja also organized a Dutch Mennonite and Quaker Relief Service during World War II, to assist refugees from Poland, Czechoslovakia and other places overrun or annexed by the Nazis. The Peace Group also helped Eberhard Arnold's people—the Society of Brothers—driven out by Hitler's Gestapo, to come to Holland and eventually resettle in Great Britain.

When war came to the Low Countries in May 1940, the Peace Group went underground but continued to be active for some time. They assisted the victims of bombed-out Rotterdam, hid Jews from the Nazi hunters, and somehow or other delivered seven hundred food parcels a week to internees inside the concentration camp of Westerbork! The Gleijsteen home was equipped with false ceilings to form hiding spaces for Jews and for Dutch intellectuals in danger of being eradicated.

Also during the mid-1930s Gleijsteen became the co-founder, along with the Quakers Kees and Betty Boeke, of a Christian school system based on the principles of brotherhood and community. In these schools the students, kindergarten through high school, were called workers, and the teachers were called co-workers. The schools had only minimal staff and no janitors. Most of the necessary tasks were performed cooperatively by the workers and co-workers after hours. At great risk the schools made an effort to educate Jewish students far into the war years.

Gleijsteen also envisioned a Christian economic system called God's Property and a credit cooperative based on barter—piano lessons for garden vegetables, shoe repair in trade for tutoring in French.

Baptized at age twenty-six, Gleijsteen fully identified with the church and participated heartily in all its functions, particularly when it came to Bible studies and peace activities. His was a familiar presence at local and regional conferences and events. He participated in six of the eleven Mennonite World Conference assemblies, beginning in 1936 and ending with Strasbourg in 1984, where, at age eighty-nine, he was reportedly the oldest registrant.[1]

Struggling with Conscription in Colombia

In Colombia, South America, each male high school graduate receives a military medical check-up. Those who pass enter a lottery which determines who is drafted into the army. About ten percent of the graduates receive a red ballot, which means that they are exempted from service. Those who receive a yellow ballot are required to report to the army in January, and those who get a blue one must report in April. In 1991, about sixty thousand young men were drafted into the army. At that time, there were no alternative service provisions for conscientious objectors, although Mennonites and others are working hard to make this possible.

Peter Stucky, executive secretary for the Mennonite church in Colombia, shares the following stories of three Mennonite young men who struggled with their military obligations.

Marcos*

Marcos finished high school in November, 1989. In the lottery drawing, he received a blue ballot, with orders to report for service the following April. "To not have a card proving completion of military service is a problem," Marcos reports. "I applied to the District University, but since I didn't have my military papers I was not admitted." Young men also need the card to get a job, to get a passport and to buy and sell property.

Not prepared to pay the consequences of publicly declaring himself a conscientious objector, Marcos chose to buy his way out of the military. This means paying off the necessary people for an exemption, usually by being declared medically unfit. A fairly common practice in Colombia, it is expensive, costing between 250 and 450 dollars. It is also risky since people are sometimes tricked out

* All names are fictitious

of their money.

Marcos' congregation has supported him throughout this experience. When several church members discussed his case, trying to sort through options, they decided that military service is such a distorting experience for a young man's personality and values that almost any other option is preferable. Since Marcos and his family did not have all the money he needed, the congregation lent him some, which he has since paid back.

Ramon

Ramon is another Mennonite youth who received a card ordering him to report to the army. On it is a quotation by Bolivar, one of Colombia's founders: "I've followed the glorious career of arms to receive the honors that they bestow: To free my country and to deserve the blessings of many peoples." Ramon ignored his summons and did not report on the stipulated date. He is now remiss and would be in serious trouble if apprehended. He tries not to get caught, which sometimes means nerve-racking close encounters with military patrols.

Like Marcos, Ramon does not want to go into the army. He explains, "Foremost is my Christian conviction, yet I also understand the dangers and risks implied in military service. In the military you're under someone else's orders." A friend of Ramon's was recruited. "He turned into a cold blooded murderer during his military service and now that he is out, he is a real menace to society," says Ramon. "Besides, it's a waste of time. My family needs me, my church too. And I need to attend to my education."

Ramon chose not to buy his way out of the military. While Marcos never questioned the practice, Ramon feels that "it's dishonest and you're paying others to lie for you." Ramon does have a contact with a high official in the Recruitment Department and hopes to obtain his military paper through this connection.

Miguel

Miguel is a third Mennonite young man drafted by the military. At the 1991 Annual Mennonite Church Convention, Miguel sought advice from us as church leaders. He said that he did not want to serve and was willing to declare himself a conscientious objector. We discussed his options, and the possibility that he might end up in the army's prison or that the commanding officer might decide not to hassle him and could give him an alternate job or maybe even send him home. We also talked about the decisions he would be facing: How far should he take his convictions? Would he put on a uniform? Would he take part in basic training? Would he not cooperate with anything?

We helped him write an affidavit explaining his position and gave him a letter to the commanding officer from the church. Then the whole assembly had special prayer for him. It was a moving occasion, and a significant moment for the church, to be confronted directly with their first conscientious objector and back him up in this way.

The next day Miguel reported to the induction center. After waiting all day at the brigade, he was declared "sobrante" (left over) and sent home. Miguel can obtain his military papers without serving and is now back home.[1]

Making it Over the Mountain

Leslie Francisco III is the pastor of a Mennonite church in Hampton, Virginia, an area which hosts a Navy shipyard and hundreds of military contractors. Approximately one-third of the people in this congregation come from families with low incomes who face limited economic opportunity. In this context, Pastor Francisco teaches that a commitment to Christ is also a step on the way to peace.

At the beginning of the Persian Gulf Crisis," recalls Pastor Francisco, "we had a prayer meeting. I asked the members of the congregation how many of them had aunts, uncles, cousins, or other close family members on military duty in the Persian Gulf. Our little congregation of 125 counted fifty-nine extended family members (none of them church members) on military duty there.

"This crisis has certainly given us a new awareness of what war is all about. People often forget about the gruesome part. They don't remember that war brings pain, suffering and grief.

"Our young people in particular are vulnerable to military recruitment at a very young age. Some of them join the Jr. ROTC (Reserve Officer Training Corp) programs in the seventh and eighth grade. They are attracted to the glitter of travel to places like California, Hawaii or other countries, and to the prospects of getting a college education through the military.

"Many of our youth come from low-income families. They live in housing projects. Every day they see drug pushers and mothers with two or three children and no husbands. Our youth look for a way to escape, and see the military as a way out."

Pastor Francisco works hard to make sure that the young people in his congregation take school seriously and consider going to college. "Our job is to help change people's mentality. People often think if someone gets through high school, they've made it over the mountain. We want our youth to develop their minds and potential first, before they consider the question of military service."

There are, however, significant obstacles to helping young people consider alternatives to military service. "The costs are perhaps the most significant. Our congregation has very limited resources, but we do offer a $250 scholarship to our youth who enroll in college. This at least gives them a sense of our support and encouragement.

"Sometimes I have to work against the counsel of parents who have military backgrounds in order to get youth to consider alternatives to the military."

Despite the best efforts of the church, there are times when youth still choose the military. Pastor Francisco notes with some sadness the recent choice of a seventeen-year-old young woman to go to Army boot camp upon graduation from high school.

"She had been coming to our church since she was about eight years old," he said. "Since she started high school, we had been encouraging her to go to college, and she responded to this counsel with enthusiasm. But a couple months ago she stopped attending church, and then told us that she had already signed up with the Army under the Delayed Entry Program.

"The Army had told her that she was a high achiever, and that she would go far in a military career. Having been in Jr. ROTC for a number of years, she also faced a lot of peer pressure to join the military. What we were encouraging her to do at church was not being reinforced in the home, or by her peers.

"Obviously, we were disappointed. It has been our experience that if young people can get into college first, other doors will open up for them, and they won't even consider the military. We don't harbor any animosity toward her."

This is characteristic of a stance of openness and welcome which the congregation takes toward people in the military. Military people who wish to become members of the church are not turned away. "We believe that through our teaching and our lifestyles, people will understand that Jesus teaches peace," notes Pastor Francisco. "We don't want people to feel alienated. We accept people into membership upon their confession of Christ as Savior. This gives them a sense of belonging. After this, they join the new members' class, and upon completion, become baptized.

"We teach that God wants us to love our enemies, and not to hate them. It's been our experience that people come to this understanding after they are with us for a time. About a year ago, one man who had been a part of the military for ten years decided to resign his post.

"We used to wait until the military recruiters contacted our young people, then begin with an onslaught of peace teaching. By that point it's too late. We discovered that we really can't start too young to begin teaching about peace. We now begin in the third or fourth grade, and teach with intensity. We have to be just as focused and proficient in our efforts as the military is.

"We have also been trying to inspire our youth with a greater commitment to mission and service. Some of our young people will be going on a three-week mission assignment to Jamaica this summer. This will help them understand that there are opportunities for service in the church which offer an alternative to the military."

Scheduled for Execution

C hristian Schmucker, a member of the Amish community, lived in Berks County, Pennsylvania during the years of the American Revolutionary War. The patriots of the area frequently accused the Amish and Mennonites of being unpatriotic or Tories (loyal to England) due to their refusal to take up arms in support of the revolution.

Because of their religious convictions against military service, Christian and several other Amish men were taken to court in Reading, and sentenced to be shot. A date was set for the execution. While Christian was in prison, his wife Catherine and their grandson carried meals to him daily. As they walked along the streets of Reading, the people of the town mocked them, and some of the town boys threw stones at them.

Henry Hertzell, a pastor in the German Reformed Church, intervened on behalf of the sentenced men and the execution was never carried out. Pastor Hertzell's appeal noted that these men had fled from Europe to escape military service, and should not now be expected to do what their consciences forbade them to do in Europe.

The authorities agreed to release Christian and his friends, but required them to buy their freedom by paying for substitutes. [1]

To Migrate or to Stay

In 1867 and 1868, Prussian Mennonites met with the Minister of War, and with His Excellency, King William I, to seek exemption from military service on the basis of their religious convictions.

Historians believe that Mennonites began settling in Prussia shortly after the establishment of the Anabaptist movement in Holland. Initially, the Mennonites of Prussia and Poland were given religious freedom and were able to remain nonresistant. In 1789, however, an edict from the king made it impossible for Mennonites to buy new land without facing military conscription. Additionally, they were required to pay yearly taxes for the support of a military school at Culm, West Prussia.[1] Wishing to remain nonresistant, some Mennonites began migrating to Russia.

As Prussian Mennonites became more integrated into Prussian society, they became less concerned with maintaining exemption from conscription. Nonetheless, as it became clear that exemption from military service might no longer be granted, a small but determined group of Mennonites did travel to Berlin to express their concerns to the king.

Record of the personal efforts of the five Mennonite elders at the high levels of state in Berlin, concerning how to avoid implementation of the country's military law which Parliament had issued over us Mennonites, November 9, 1867.

We five elders started our journey on October 3, 1867, via railroad to Berlin, where we stayed at the Alexander Hotel. Thereafter we went to Kastlan Gutklee at the Department of Trade who was a known and good friend to us. As a Christian believer he was always helpful to us, because he had knowledge of all things, and he was also known everywhere in the Department. We had daily audiences with him as long as we were in Berlin.

On the 24th of October, we went to Herrn von Brauchitsch, who welcomed us. He informed us of the many things on the mind of the high government. At two o'clock p.m., Mr. von Brauchitsch had arranged a meeting for us with His Excellency, Herrn von Roon, the Minister of War. The High Lord welcomed us frankly. After Brother Tows explained our miserable situation and asked for us to be exempt from this law, the High Lord said

it would not be his authority to exempt us from the military law, but we should not worry, everything would turn out right. He recommended that we should show our respect by offering to serve in the medical units. He hoped that this would be acceptable.

I asked if this service would include the carrying of weapons. He answered, "We cannot do without the carrying of a hand gun. Even if it would not be used, it should be carried to honor the king." I replied that in this case, we would have to deny even this service, because the carrying of weapons is against our religious beliefs.

After this His Excellence engaged us in a deep conversation about our pacifism. Finally, His Excellence posed a serious question, with the words, "What do you think about us using weapons in war, concerning the salvation of our souls?" As he was asking this, His Excellency was very close to me with two fingers holding onto my suit.

I felt pressured to answer, and replied with the help of God, "Your Excellence, we see it similar to the Apostle Paul's writing to the Corinthians about pagan sacrifices. When the church bought meat at the market, they should buy what was offered, but if it was told to them that it would be a sacrificed meat, they should not buy it, because it would cause them to sin. We see military service in the same way.

"We were told by our parents and by our spiritual leaders out of the word of God that war is sin. We sucked in these beliefs with our mother's milk, and so it became a burden for our conscience. If we then go to war, it is sin for us. Your Excellence and your colleagues were taught that waging war and protecting your home country is a holy duty. This you also learned as you drank your mother's milk. Thus it is not adultery. Therefore what became sin to us is not sin to you."

His Highness replied, "So you let our kind into heaven too?" I said, "Well sure." His Excellence replied, "Now I am satisfied." He left us with the hope that he would do everything in his power to solve our problem, and he dismissed us with a handshake.

In September of 1868, this same delegation returned to Berlin, and met the king and crown prince in two separate audiences.

These meetings were inconclusive, granting Mennonites the opportunity to perform noncombatant medical service, but not permitting total exemption from military duty. Some Mennonites stayed in Prussia, while other migrated to the Ukraine in search of greater freedom of conscience.[2]

Making Toys, Not Grenades

The year was 1940. Jake Brubaker, a toy designer, wood turner and minister in the Mennonite church was employed by the Hubley Toy Company in Lancaster, Pennsylvania. As World War II began to sweep across continents, Jake was busy designing toy wagons and automobiles for children.

Even in the relative seclusion of a toy factory surrounded by rich farmland in rural Pennsylvania, Jake could not long avoid a clear invitation to join the war effort. Confronted by an army general clutching blueprints for grenades, Jake had to decide the ultimate purpose of the work of his hands.

Jake's career as a toy maker began in 1912, when he first began to work for Hubley Toy Company, a cast iron toy manufacturer. While Jake began as an assembler, Hubley soon noticed his natural gift for tinkering and gave him a room to himself just for designing new toys. In one year, Jake designed sixty-seven new toys.

In the following excerpts from an oral history interview conducted by Paul Brubaker in 1979, Jake describes his work at Hubley Toy Company during the war years.

Jake: About 1940, when the war broke out, Hubley had to stop making toys because they had to go into defense work.

Paul: What did they make?

Jake: Oh they made float lights. For instance, if a ship got torpedoed, an airplane would fly out over the area where the ship had sunk, and drop a lot of float lights that float on the ocean and burn for quite a few hours. It was some kind of a magnesium flare. Hubley also made a fuze, a detonator which the Army used to put in the bottom of a gas tank. As long as the safety pin wasn't pulled, it was safe. But in case the vehicle would fall into the hands of the enemy, they were supposed to pull that pin, and then anybody that moved it would blow up the tank. I have some of them laying around here some place, those detonators.

Paul: You worked for Hubley all through those years too?

Jake: Well, when the war broke out, there were some generals who came in from Philadelphia, because Hubley had a big foundry—eighty-eight or ninety molders, and they wanted Hubley to make hand grenades, you know those kinds that explode into pieces and kill a man, and are anti-personnel.

So the president, Mr. Brenneman, called me in and introduced me to the generals that came there from the army and said, "Jake, (see, I was the head toy designer) meet General 'So-and-So.' General 'So-and-So' says they have a blueprint here for you to look at and make up."

I looked at it and passed it back to him. It was a blueprint for a hand grenade. I said, "I'm sorry Mr. Brenneman, but I have compunctions of conscience to make that thing, because that's for the destruction of life. You ask me to make something for the preservation of life, why I'll do it, but I have a concience on making a hand grenade."

So they dismissed me, and they called in another man from the pattern shop, and he took over in my place. I was going to quit, but Mr. Brenneman said, "Now Jake, what are you going to do? You know, the country is at war. We're all in it. You'll have to do something. Everybody, even the farmer that raises cattle and produces milk, he's helping in the war effort."

I said, "Yes, but that's for the preservation of life. When it comes to making hand grenades, that's different. That's taking a man's life."

He said, "What are you going to do?"

I said, "Well, I don't worry, I'll fix rocking chairs or something. I'll find something to do."

"Well no," he said, "we don't want you to quit."

He said, "I heard of a man up in Copiague, Long Island. He's a German that has a formula for making toys out of wood flour, and he wants to sell it to us to make toys out of material that is non-strategic. Now Hubley can make all the toys they want, providing they didn't use any steel or strategic materials, you know, iron."

So he and I went up on the train to Copiague, Long Island, and there they were making umbrella handles out of this material. They'd take wood flour and mix different ingredients, and that plasticized it. They would put it under a press and press it into a mold, and take it out to dry. Then it was hard like a piece of wood. You could drill it, machine it and paint it. So we designed a bunch of pull toys. One was a lamb, one was a dog, and there were different animals. Each one had four little wood wheels on it, and a pull string.

We set up a pilot workshop outside of the plant to make these animals. They made millions and millions of these things during the war because Mr. Brenneman wanted to keep the name of the Hubley Company before the public until the war was over. So he put me at the head of that to produce this formula.

Hubley only made a few samples of hand grenades, but then they didn't go into production. They made these float lights and they made fuses for these gas tanks you know. And they made iron castings for some kind of a device they used in Europe during the war to drop down and light up an area. They were making those things, but my occupation in the Hubley Company was this plastic toy business.

No Longer a Warrior

Joseph Sangale is a Maasai church leader in Kenya. Baptized as a youth in the Maranatha Mission church, he joined the Mennonite church in Ogwedi, Kenya in 1988.

In February, 1984, some cows belonging to Joseph's neighbor Mapengo, were stolen by the Kuria. When the alarm cry went out, Joseph picked up his bow, a quiver of arrows, a spear, and a short sword, and joined his clansmen in hot pursuit. They followed the tracks of the cows about twenty kilometers to Ekirage, deep inside Kuria land. There the tracks dispersed and disappeared in the tall grass.

As was the custom, the police and the chief were called to witness the end of the trail. The people in this community would be held accountable and would be forced to produce the stolen cattle or an equivalent number to replace them. Leaving the matter in the hands of the police and the local chief and elders, most of the Maasai warriors returned home.

Several stayed behind, however, to write an official statement for the police. This group included Joseph, as the one who had gone to school; Mapengo, the owner of the cattle; and Ole Kosiom, a friend. Suddenly they were three Maasai warriors alone in the heart of enemy territory. A band of drunk Kuria took notice and began to shoot arrows at them. They were hopelessly outnumbered. Fighting back would be suicide. They sought refuge in the person of the Kuria chief by running in circles around him, while the Kuria continued shooting at them. The chief could not stop the drunken mob, so he ran with the three Maasai and took them to the shelter of a nearby house and locked them inside until the police could come. They stayed there all night.

In that house that night, Joseph Sangale thought deeply about the matter of killing. He could have easily shot someone in pure self-defense in that moment of skirmish. But what would Jesus think of him had he done so? Did Jesus defend himself when he was being arrested, tried and crucified? If Jesus did not defend himself, should he? What about that commandment that says, "Do not kill"? If a Christian is a follower of Jesus and is dedicated to doing the will of God, can he really kill in self-defense? Can he even threaten to kill as a means of self-defense? If the answer is "No," then why was he here with weapons?

The next morning Joseph and his friends returned home. Joseph went out and starting shooting his arrows into the forest. His brother came along and thought he was going mad. He took Joseph's quiver and remaining arrows away from him. Then Joseph broke his bow and threw it into the bush. Joseph says that was the point of his real conversion, when he really decided to trust God for his protection, and to follow Christ in the new way of defenseless love.

Still alone in his faith and a bit unsure, Joseph did carry a symbolic spear on later stolen cattle chases, but he resolved never to use it. Several years later, he was given the booklet, What Mennonites Believe,[1] by J.C. Wenger. He discussed the teaching on biblical nonresistance with his friend and brother in Christ, Francis Ole Rekei. They both agreed to be completely nonresistant and asked to join the Mennonite Church later that year.

Today, Joseph still joins his warrior neighbors in following the tracks of stolen cattle. But he carries only a long walking stick and his Bible. The neighbors mock him, but let him come along with them. He reminds them that he is protected by God.

At times his aged mother ridicules him: "You ought to wear a skirt. You don't have any weapons in your house. You don't even go and help your age-mates in their war against the Siriya. You haven't even stolen one cow from the Luo. Even I am a better man than you!"

Joseph has conceded that he does not know if he could remain nonresistant if he had a strong father to oppose him. His father died before Joseph was born. Other young men have strong fathers and in Maasai culture the pressure to honor one's father is extreme. The culturally appropriate way to honor one's father is to become a great warrior like Joseph used to be, by collecting the largest herd of cattle (mainly by stealing), by protecting those cattle from would-be thieves, by killing the most enemies in times of theft or war and by being the bravest and cleverest fighter when helping neighbors retrieve their stolen cattle.[2]

The 1919 Petition

In 1919, several bills on compulsory military training came before the Congress of the United States. None of the bills provided exemption for conscientious objectors. In response, the Mennonite Church Peace Problems Committee wrote a petition to Congress, asking for consideration for nonresistant Christians. This petition was circulated among Mennonites, with a cover letter from the Mennonite General Conference Executive Committee (not to be confused with the present day General Conference Mennonite Church). The letter noted that Congress was considering compusory military training legislation, and urged church members to sign the petition which appears below. It was signed by twenty thousand Mennonites in thirty-one states.

Believing all war to be a violation of the teachings of Christ whose life and precepts we hold as our supreme law, we feel that we must also avoid having any part in Military Training, therefore we, the undersigned, humbly plead your Honorable body that it pass no laws which will force militarism upon those who have religious convictions against it. We are confident that the passing of Military Laws which would not excuse non-resistant Christians would mean to send thousands of young men to Military Prisons and no good government desires this."

Signed by 20,000 Mennonites[1]

Lessons about Enemies

Marian Claassen Franz, director of the National Campaign for a Peace Tax Fund, grew up in a Mennonite family in rural Kansas. A child during World War II, she recalls the following contacts with the "enemy."

Mother's explosive "Thank God!" revealed the contents of the letter from the draft board. A farm deferment meant that my only brother would not have to leave home. We did not usually stop work just because the mail had arrived, but today we paused to reflect on our good fortune.

Shortly, however, our minds concentrated on the tragic news in that same day's mail, as each day the newspapers displayed photos of fine young men who were being killed in World War II. Not mourned in the local press were the thousands of injuries and deaths of enemy soldiers and civilians.

Those victims consumed a good deal of our attention during the war years. My family received a succession of letters from Europeans who had no access to a relief agency, and desperately needed clothing and other basic supplies. We carefully cataloged their letters and requests for help.

Shopping to fill their requests, we plunged into tables full of secondhand clothing and walked into large department stores, where we were personally greeted by the managers who had laid aside seconds for us, discounted some prices, and who tried to accommodate our large orders for such items as long underwear in such large amounts.

Packing days among the several families that participated in the effort were exciting. Each completed package seemed to reflect the personality of the persons to whom they were sent, as we laid in shoes, baby clothes, tins of food, socks, coats, sweaters, long underwear and coffee. Coffee was a rarity in war-time Europe, and was valuable as barter for other necessities. So were cigarettes, but we never sent them.

I learned even more powerful lessons, too. During World War II, there were German soldiers in the busy harvest fields of my Kansas childhood home. These prisoners of war were housed in a small nearby town, and were available to work on local farms during the day.

I was not afraid of these enemy soldiers. What terrified me were the U.S. guards who accompanied them. They were the ones with the guns. In total terror I watched as one demonstrated how to attach his bayonet to the end of a gun barrel. No gun intended to kill people or to spear stomachs had ever before been near our home.

At first the guards were tense, the prisoners wary. At noontime on the first day, after washing up out of doors with the rest of the harvesters, they waited outside to be served. Perhaps the prisoners expected to be served out of doors from tin cans? My mother stepped onto the porch and in perfect German invited them in to her table as graciously as she would have any other guests. Overcome by the unexpected kindness, several wept.

As time passed, the tension between the German and U.S. soldiers was eroded on both sides by the hospitality that our Mennonite home and community extended equally to friend and foe. Guards no longer brought their dreaded guns to the table (to my enormous relief), but left them out on the porch. After meals, we all gathered around the piano to sing hymns and folk songs in both German and English. These enemies, who in other circumstances would have been shooting each other, swapped photos and stories of their families back home. My father translated the jokes they wanted to tell each other. I remember one about Italian tanks that had four speeds in reverse. Not knowing of Italy's brief participation in the war, I did not understand what was funny.

One afternoon, to escape the broiling Kansas sun the single guard for that day had gone to nap under the shady trees along the creek, leaving the prisoners alone with the farmers. Suddenly excited chatter erupted amid a frantic flurry of activity. The prisoners had spied a fast-approaching army jeep with its load of military superiors coming to inspect the guard on duty. Several prisoners rushed to the creek to waken the guard, who hastily rubbed the sleep from his eyes and regained his watchful post. There were stiff salutes, the clatter of weapons inspection, some intense conversation. Satisfied that the prisoners would not escape under such vigilant watch, the officers boarded their jeep and disappeared as quickly as they had arrived.

The silent tension of the field broke into explosive laughter as guards and prisoners alike enjoyed the success of that close call.

What was a little girl to think? If the German and U.S. soldiers were not each other's enemies, who was the enemy in the war that was killing and maiming so many people? Had the soldiers of these warring countries not made common cause against the real enemy—the system of war?

When the awful war was finally over, my parents visited the enemy country and the enemy families—both the recipients of the packages and former prisoners. In one home, they joked that our family picture had been displayed just for this visit. Almost angrily, the woman retorted, "Das bild steht immer am ehren platz!" ("That picture stands continually in a place of honor!") She insisted they would not have survived the dreadful war years without our help.

Another family honored my parents in another way. The family had saved a treasured can of coffee, received in one of those packages, for some very special event. My parents' visit provided that occasion. How could my parents ever have dreamed when they packed that coffee, that they would sit down and drink it together with the recipients!

I have not forgotten the childhood lessons. Enemies, I have since noted, come and go with considerable speed. In the past half century Germany, Japan, and China have turned from being U.S. friend to enemy and back again. The Soviet Union reversed that cycle: foe, friend, foe.

Exaggerated fear of Soviet enemies is used to create disproportionate military budgets and provide defense contracts for large corporations. Are those who would inflate our fears and who stand to make huge profits not really as afraid of the enemy as they want us to be?

I am thankful for the childhood lessons about enemies. I am proud that our people were not like thermometers that automatically rise and fall with every manipulation of popular hatreds. Rather, they were like thermostats which help to moderate the irrational fears that take potential friends to war.

The Way of Peace in a Football Game

My father was a professional boxer, who late in life joined the Mennonite Church. When I was a kid, he showed me how to fight, and made it clear that he didn't want to see me running away from a fight. He saw me do that one day, and got into my world in a very personal way real fast. 'Next time I see you run away, you'll have to fight me,' he said."

Raymond Jackson grew up in North Philadelphia, Pennsylvania, where intimidation and violence were a part of the world of the street. Blessed with a large physique, Raymond was not often challenged by his peers. Nonetheless, he struggled to find a balance between his father's push toward confrontation, and his mother's pacifism.

From his youth, Raymond attended Diamond Street Mennonite Church, located in the heart of North Philadelphia. It was known as the "Come To Jesus Church," because of the words painted on the cross which hung from the church's second story. When Raymond came to Jesus as a youth, the issue of Jesus' way of peace was significant for him.

"There were gangs on the street. I remember one time on the way home from church I met a twelve-year-old kid who had a sawed-off shotgun under his coat. The policemen were scared of kids like this. In that environment, I felt that if you turned one cheek and then the other, you might be dead. It was fine for the church to talk about not fighting, but it didn't feel like there was much substance to it. The people who talked about peace and reconciliation didn't know how to fight anyway. It felt like a position of weakness rather than strength.

"The Cuban missile crisis happened when I was fifteen or sixteen years of age. I was very patriotic then. When I heard Kennedy speak, I knew I was ready to go fight if I was needed.

"When I became a member of the church, I had some problems with the issue of conscientious objection. I became a member clearly stating that I didn't buy that position. But I also agreed that as a 'follower of Jesus,' I would read and study, so that by the time a draft came along, I could rightfully claim conscientious objector status as my own belief.

"By the time I was eighteen years old, I did register as a conscientious objector. My draft board was shocked. I was called in to explain myself. They didn't ask me to defend or explain my convictions, but I did have to show how I got them. They couldn't understand how a fellow that grew up in the environment of North Philadelphia could have these beliefs."

Raymond readily acknowledges the influence of his parents and his own study on his convictions. However, it was a football game at Camp Hebron, a Mennonite campground, which helped him clarify his thinking.

"We had a long football game one day, and I was playing hard and rough. I played opposite this 'country bumpkin,' and I beat him all day long. Every time we got to the line he was there, and I whipped him. He was frustrated. At the end of the day I was feeling bad about the way I had treated him. When I looked at him, I realized that if I had been in his position, we would have been fighting. But not once had he tried to get even with me that day. I realized that he responded to my treatment graciously, not because of his character, but because Jesus reigned supreme in his life. It was his walk with Jesus that made the difference.

"Through that game, and through thinking about Jesus' call to turn the other cheek, I made my commitment to follow in Jesus' way of peace. After I registered as a conscientious objector, I signed up for Voluntary Service, and went to serve in Atlanta, Georgia."

Today, Raymond lives with his family in North Philadelphia. As he watches his fifteen-year-old son, he wonders how to instill a commitment to Christ's way of peace in his life.

"We have drugs in our neighborhood. We hear gunshots almost every night, related to drugs. My children are witnesses to this almost daily. I pray that they don't become a part of it."

In addition to the violence on the streets, Raymond is also concerned about the way children in his neighborhood become enamored with military violence.

"Recently there was a story in the news about the visit of military recruiters to a local school. They had an air force pilot there who put on his equipment in front of the kids, and also had one of the kids wear it. Now this kid is sure he wants to be an airplane pilot. I don't know how well he can read and write, but he wants to be a pilot. It angers me that ghetto kids are treated in this way."

While Raymond is concerned for his children, he also discovers that there are ways to witness to peace in his own life. In many American communities during the Persian Gulf War, individuals wore small flags, yellow ribbons, or bracelets to show support for the U.S. troops in the Middle East. This issue confronted Raymond on the job.

"One of the managers brought in flags for everyone to wear, and another employee brought in bracelets. Now as big as I am, I could have beat up everybody, but I didn't have the power to change their minds. I told them that I cannot support violence against anybody, and that there is a better way to work at our problems. They were surprised by my attitude, and haven't asked me to do anything else.

"Our world and our ghettos function in the same way—by violence. We need a 'Youth Peace Corps' to provide an alternative to this violence, and demonstrate a better way."

From Military Service to Christian Nonresistance

During the nineteenth century and more particularly just before the first World War, military service became obligatory for all twenty-one-year-old French men. With some exceptions, most French Mennonites began to perform military service like everybody else.

In this atmosphere Pierre Widmer, a French Mennonite, was raised. But his renewed study of the scriptures and later position as a French military officer during World War II, caused a real struggle of conscience for Pierre.

I remember our children's games, during and after the other war. We had seen so much of soldiers that most of our games were games having to do with war. I often played a commander, wearing stripes on my cap and on my sleeves, and I used to dream of really wearing them someday. To be an officer in the French army, the finest in the world: what an ideal!"

Before entering college, Pierre became troubled with the nature of his relationship to God, and spent a great deal of time studying the Bible. "As I began to comprehend the love of God for me, I also was discovering the horror of sin, and of war, which is one of sin's particularly frightful manifestations. I became more and more convinced that my boyhood dream was incompatible with a true Christian life. Would I never be able to be an officer?

"In 1928, I entered the normal school for teachers at Besancon, and, like all my comrades, I began to take advanced military training to become a reserve officer. But my conscience would not rest, and after two or three months, I discontinued it under the pretext that my health was not very good, and that my studies gave me enough to do. This was not the real reason. It was hard for me to have to say that I didn't like to do my military service, and I had not yet decided to refuse absolutely to bear arms.

"At that time various pacifist movements were influencing opinion in our country, and I remember having actively participated in different meetings in behalf of peace. I did not wish at all to help in preparing for war by performing my military service. However, as a teacher, I had to teach obedience to the laws of my country and to be an example: I had to do my military service.

"In 1933 I had been deferred by the examining board. In 1934, when I went before it again, the president of the examining board spoke of deferring me again because of a 'weak constitution.' I declared that I had never been sick. He said aloud 'Good for the armed services!' The die was cast, and it was a relief for me, for I disliked having to pass again as unfit for military service.

"But when, in the spring of 1935, I arrived at the barracks, I had fully made up my mind to do everything I could in order not to have to bear arms. I explained to my officer that I wanted to be a good citizen and to serve my country well, but that because of conscientious scruples, I did not wish to bear arms. I asked to serve as a nurse in the company made up of soldiers without rank. He answered that if I wanted to serve my country well, I could do nothing better than to give an example of obedience and become an officer, as my capabilities bade me do. There was no other way for me.

"I returned to my barracks room and fell to my knees to ask God to help me and to show me the way. Here I must candidly recognize that I was afraid to carry out my desire to be obedient to Christ. If I deliberately renounced becoming an officer, if I refused to follow the preparatory course, what would happen? I would immediately be regarded with disfavor, prohibited from continuing such a course of action, considered a Communist and an antimilitarist, a bad Frenchman, and I would undoubtedly find it hard to continue in my profession. Beyond that, I was anxious for the esteem of men and for preserving my good reputation, and it was terribly painful for me to renounce these. Certainly I was evading the issue. I had not truly made up my mind to obey God rather than men."

After some additional soul-searching, Pierre decided to return to school, and completed his officer's training. In the build-up to World War II, however, Pierre became more and more distressed with his status.

"I was troubled at the thought of war and that I, a Mennonite, was to be an officer, and that I would without doubt have to command the firing."

Upon completion of his training, Pierre did find himself in the firing line. "I am in Alsace, September, 1939, at the end of the Maginot Line, and we are working hard to put into good condition whatever part of the front we can. Already people speak of an eventual attack with gas. Certainly we are not attacking, and we are here only in a position of defense. My uneasy conscience tries to satisfy itself with this truth: we are not aggressors. We are taking up arms solely to come to the aid of the small nations eaten up by the monster, and to prevent eventual aggression against our own country.

"But the sight which torments me exceedingly is that of the evacuation of the Alsatian population, the mournful passing by of these thousands and thousands of people. I want to help them, to show them a little kindness! But what can I do? I am an officer, and I do not have the time to look after them. However, I feel myself made more for such work than for the work of a soldier. There are enough others who respond to the call of violence. And I feel like a stranger among them.

"But May 10, 1940 arrives, bringing the brutal aerial attack of the Germans on Holland, Belgium, and France. Several days afterwards I am in Alsace, at the border of the Rhine in the Haardt forest. In the morning the planes pass again in successive waves high overhead. It is absolutely useless to fire on them with our infantry weapons. But I am suddenly seized with an intense feeling of revolt: they are not attacking us, the soldiers, the people prepared to fight, but our wives, our children, our parents, our friends, our villages, our schools, our homes, and I want to do something to prevent them from doing it. I seize the machine gun, in firing position on its picket. I take aim. I fire, but the charge does not go off. The weapon locks—it is impossible to fire with this machine gun. And there I am, my feeling of revolt in my heart, and my useless weapon in my hands. God is speaking to me. It is not given to me to use these weapons of war to accomplish justice according to the opinion of men."

Six months later, during the last days of the French campaign, Pierre was taken prisoner with his whole army. He was imprisoned, and held captive for five years. "In 1935 I was afraid of going to prison. I shrank in the face of this prospect. I did not accept this dishonor entailed in loving Christ and remaining faithful to the Gospel. And now I do not have the choice. I am a prisoner and am going to be one for a long time.

"Prompted by loyalty, I tried to be a child of peace with weapons in my hand, not for attacking other people, but for defending my own. And I did not succeed. Now I want to count on God and leave to Him the care of defending us, my people and myself, as He has promised."[1]

B-52 Brakes on My Workbench

Jeff didn't know what to do. There on the workbench in front of him were magnesium brake parts for B-52 bombers. The parts had been returned for minor repairs to the machine shop where he worked. Jeff's job was to lightly sand the beveled edges.

It was the fall of 1980. "I had just spent almost all my money on a trip to Ireland," recalls Jeff. "I planned to work for a year to earn enough money to continue college. So I eagerly accepted a machine shop job that paid $6.25 an hour with ten hours overtime a week.

"I had grown up in a Mennonite community in the U.S. where nonresistance wasn't a radical idea, but an almost expected belief. I learned pacifism at home, in Sunday school and even from the preacher, if I tried to follow the sermon. Instead of World War II stories, Dad told us Civilian Public Service stories. When other kids told their fathers' tales, I told them my father was a "guinea pig" during the war as part of his alternate service project. Nobody else had a dad that was used for a pneumonia experiment. I grew up without having to prove my beliefs. There was no draft registration when I turned eighteen, so I wasn't forced to deal with practical pacifism.

"In 1980, Congress threatened to reinstate the draft. Nonresistance became a real issue. I struggled over a Christian Peacemaker Registration form, two green sheets of paper with five impossible questions. One asked how my belief affected the type of work I will do to earn a living. How would I answer if a judge scowled at me over his walnut throne and asked what I believed and why? I could hear him say, 'Do you really believe that, or are you trying to get out of being drafted?'"

That Friday afternoon in September, the other employees laughed and joked with each other, glad for the break from heavier work.

Jeff's response was different. "As my fingers worked on the brake parts, my conscience worked on my mind. According to my answers on the Christian Peacemaker Registration form, each stroke of my arm aided the military I refused to serve.

"As I drove home, I wondered if I should have refused to work on the brake parts. They were only a small piece of a big machine that dropped bombs, I reasoned with myself. I only contributed an hour and a half of my entire life to lightly sanding a tiny edge of that small part. Besides, they were all finished and there would be no more to worry about."

Much to Jeff's surprise, there were more brake parts to be sanded on Monday morning. Jeff resolved to go see his boss and explain why he could not in good conscience do the work assigned to him.

"It took two false starts and a trip to the water fountain to get myself to the boss's office," remembers Jeff. "I explained my beliefs as briefly and as best I could."

Jeff's boss, also a Mennonite, was not amused. "He began by telling me he didn't think pacifism could hold water in the real world. Then he proceeded to lecture me on the gaps between the theory and actual practice of nonresistance: when we pay income tax we're donating to the armed forces. Any work I might do could contribute to the military. 'You may as well go back to Ohio and farm,' he said. 'But you'd better not sell any milk to the dairy because they might sell it to a general somewhere.'

"He asked how I would work to my fullest potential and be successful if I wouldn't touch anything that might indirectly be used for violent purposes. I thought of Paul's admonishment, 'Follow my example as I follow the example of Christ.'

"'Was Christ a failure?' My question surprised us both.

"'Are you equating yourself with Christ?' he asked sharply.

"'No. But this business of being successful—do you think Christ was a failure?'

"'Well. . .yes, in a sense. I don't think he accomplished what he came to earth to accomplish.'

"He continued his lecture, and I listened politely. He left me with a choice: work on the parts or leave. Leaving meant facing unemployment on a dwindling savings account and possibly giving up school for an entire year. I knew what I had to do. I punched my time card and closed the door behind me for the last time.

"'You mean you quit a $340 a week job because of a little B-52 part?' people asked. At least it's a new question."

Student Soldiers

In the fall of 1988, Ted Koontz, a Mennonite worker in the Philippines, visited a group of Burmese students who had fled violent military oppression, and were camped along the Thai-Burmese border. As a Mennonite seminary professor, Ted is a convinced pacifist, and no stranger to courses in peace theology. Confronted with rows of young students dressed in military fatigues, however, Ted found himself groping for words.

The students had fled the cities of Burma when a nationwide strike and massive pro-democracy demonstrations were brutally crushed by the Burmese Army. Thousands of protestors were killed. In the jungle, the students joined forces with ethnic insurgents who had been waging wars of independence against the military government of Burma for more than twenty years.

All the time I was at the hot, ramshackle camp on the border of Burma, my mind kept flashing back to two images from my liberal arts education. One was of Don Quixote, the hopelessly naive and idealistic knight created by Cervantes. The other was of the Children's Crusade. I could not recall details about them, but they floated through my mind. This experience too felt like a dream—a bad dream.

The camp was "home" to six hundred students who had fled from Rangoon and other cities after the military had brutally repressed their demonstrations for democracy in 1988. We drove right to it, albeit after wandering around on back roads for about an hour and a half in order to avoid border checkpoints, the last part on a trail with powdery dust about two inches deep.

We arrived at noon. The air was absolutely still, stifling. At times the cicadas in the dusty trees made normal conversation impossible. The buildings were makeshift bamboo structures mostly with no sides and with roofs made of powder dry leaves or thin blue plastic sheets, often ripped, (but still perfect for identifying the camp to the

Burmese Air Force). They were uncomfortably cold at night, I discovered, even in the dry season. They were dangerously cold during the rainy season.

More nightmarish than the setting were the students. Not that they were unpleasant. Far from it. They simply did not fit their setting. They were young, out of place in the jungle. Some were thirteen or fourteen, most were around eighteen. Few of the girls looked more than sixteen. They were city kids and belonged in school.

Our translators were English literature majors, more at home discussing T. S. Eliot than waging a revolution. Others were medical students, historians, biologists or secondary students.

Their food was inadequate. Their blue roofs exposed them to bombardment. They were subject to manipulation by outside groups on whom they had to rely for survival, groups often more interested in their own purposes than the students' welfare.

Many were sick. Infirmaries, one for males and one for females, were staffed by a veterinarian and students with a year or two of medical training. They housed perhaps fifteen students, most hooked to IVs, some looking very ill indeed. Most had stomach disorders and a serious type of malaria that is resistant to most anti-malarial medicines. "We've all had malaria at one time or another," one of them told me. A number died of it.

Clearly, in one way, none of them belonged here or really knew what they were getting into when they came here. They were school kids who wanted to be leading the ordinary lives of school kids. School kids plopped into the middle of a remote jungle.

Yet in another way, the students belonged. They had come here to escape the murder they had seen wreaked upon their friends and to avenge those murders; to overthrow the military dictatorship that rules the main part of Burma and to build a new democratic Burma. When they told their stories and spoke of what the regime had done, their hardness and firmness of purpose suddenly made them seem older than I.

While we visited with a group of students, a friend who regularly visited them asked what he could do for them when he came again. After a long silence a girl, sick with malaria, who looked no more than fifteen, answered earnestly, "Bring me an M-16." He shrugged and laughed. They knew he would not provide arms. Yet an M-16 is what they wanted most.

Yes, when they wore their ordinary clothes, when they spoke

about themselves, their lives, their interests, the horrors they had seen in Burma's cities and towns, when they cried as they remembered the taken-for-granted joys of student life—then they were school kids. But when they put on their uniforms, marched in units around the drill field, and shouted their responses to orders—or when they slithered through the jungle in their guerrilla war training—then they were revolutionaries who belonged in the jungle.

Yet even this belonging had a mixed-up, dream-like quality to it.

We are sitting in a small snack shop having soft drinks, while the main military strategist in the camp describes his plan to build a hang glider. He will, he says, jump off a cliff and sail over the Burmese military, raining hand grenades on them. Others laugh, helping me keep my grip on reality, but he is deadly serious. The next day when we leave he has most of the hang glider built. He wants us to stay for his first test flight later that afternoon.

I wonder why they think they can survive, re-entering in armed groups of perhaps ten or so, when a number of their unarmed friends have been captured and killed by the military as they sought to return. With arms they will certainly be much more conspicuous. I have an overwhelming sense of sadness. Children, I fear, walking to the slaughter.

The nightmare quality of my visit reached its peak the last morning when I was asked to speak to the students. The people before me were not students. They were now soldiers dressed in combat fatigues, standing in neat rows with their companies, shouting responses to their officers' commands, standing at attention as I spoke. I understood their anguish and their rage. I agreed with the justice of their cause. But I, a Christian pacifist, hated war. I had never been in a military training camp in my life. I thought they were wrong both morally and strategically in undertaking a guerrilla war. I feared that most of them would die senselessly. What could I say? How could they possibly understand both my support and my profound disagreement?

While I have left the nightmarish camp of my friends, I still worry about them and the choices and dangers they face. But I worry more about the nightmare that is bigger than that camp and those student-soldiers. The nightmare is regimes that push students to make the choices and face the dangers they do. The nightmare is a world that does so little to force such regimes to treat their citizens humanely. The nightmare is those of us who believe in peace, who long for peace, who work for peace, but who have so little to say or offer to those like the student-soldiers who desperately seek an alternative to armed struggle, but see none.

Perhaps the nightmare does not need to be. But to stop it we, who have more options than those students on the border, must rouse ourselves from our comfortable slumber and help create alternatives to a slaughter already underway, and to a bigger slaughter in the making.[1]

Nonresistance under Test

"Our church taught that it is wrong to engage in strife, that Christians should follow the footsteps of Jesus. But the church also taught that we should pray for rulers, pay taxes, and be good, law-abiding citizens." Emanuel Swartzendruber, a Mennonite young man, struggled to practice these teachings in the midst of World War I, under the pressure of a military draft.

Emanuel received his call to report for military service on March 4, 1918. He and seventeen others boarded the train at Bad Axe, Michigan for the long trip to Fort Oglethorpe, Georgia.

At his assigned unit, Emanuel took his first opportunity to explain his religious beliefs and convictions against war to his commanding officer. The officer was understanding, and respected Emanuel's refusal to wear the uniform or participate in drills. Emanuel also declined kitchen duty, saying, "I am not opposed to work, but I can't be a member of the army."

After several weeks, Emanuel was transferred to another company where the presiding officer had successfully forced another conscientious objector (CO) to wear the military uniform. He expected the same results with Emanuel, and tried hard to force his cooperation.

The sergeant ordered me to put on a uniform. At the same time, another young man appeared on the scene without a uniform. I made no effort to put mine on. But between kicks and cuffs I received, I could see that he didn't put his on either. Finally, the soldiers forced part of the uniforms on us.

"Get your breakfast. We'll have some fun later," the sergeant told us. By the time breakfast was over there were four COs. We were taken outside and asked to tear down an outhouse. The first thing I knew, someone grabbed me by the seat of my pants. My head struck the roof of the building. I don't know what happened—boards were flying everywhere. After the building was removed, the sergeant said, "Now we'll show you what your Jesus can do when you are in our hands."

So he threw one of the boys into the cesspool. He stood in the filth nearly up to his armpits. They took a shovel and shoveled excrement on his head saying, "I baptize you in the name of Jesus."

One of them, looking upwards said, "Can you see Jesus?"

The sergeant told us, "If he is your brother, pull him out." We pulled him out, took him to the bathhouse and cleaned him.

The the sergeant threw soap at me and pushed me into a corner, choking me. He said, "Come with me." I followed him to the cesspool. He asked me three times if I was ready to accept military service. I answered only once, "No."

He took me by my legs and put me into the cesspool head first. I heard the soldiers yelling, "Don't put him in any further, you'll kill him!"

The sergeant pulled me out, not saying a word. He stood shaking his head while I lay on the ground. Finally he said, "Go and wash."

We were taken before a group of higher officers, and asked who we were and what denomination we belonged to. The spokesman told the sergeant, "Put these men on bread and water."

We went to our stalls. As I sat on my bunk, the sergeant came to us and asked, "Do you still love me?"

I said, "Yes, I do." He walked away from me.

After the military saw that we had not changed our minds while in the guard house, they told us that we would be court-martialed. They ordered a general court-martial to be held at Camp Forrest on June 11, 1918. Eight COs were court-martialed and sentenced to prison at Fort Leavenworth, Kansas, for ten years of hard labor, forfeiting all payments and allowances.

En route to Fort Leavenworth by train, we were detained in a Memphis jail for several hours.

The jailor soon asked us why we were prisoners. After we told him, he said, "That's strange. We put people in jail because they fight and you are here because you think it is wrong to fight. If we all believed as you, we wouldn't need this jail at all."

On the way to Kansas I had a nice visit with the sergeant. He said, "When you were first put in the guard house, I thought you were nothing but war dodgers. Since watching you day by day, I have changed my mind. I used to be a Sunday School boy, but could it be possible that you are right and all the rest of us are wrong about war? I hope they treat you well at Fort Leavenworth."

Two months later the armistice was signed and I was released.[1]

We Are Ready to Serve as Substitutes

During the Vietnam War, some young Americans fled to Canada rather than face induction into the U.S. military and potential duty in Vietnam. When the war ended, the fate of these young men became a divisive political issue.

In the fall of 1974, President Ford presented his program of earned re-entry for these Vietnam-era draft law violators. Eight young women responded with the following letter:

Dear Mr. President:

We are writing out of concern for the men who acted on their convictions against violence and war, in particular an illegal and immoral war in Southeast Asia. These men, at the present time, are not even allowed to visit family and friends in the United States, whether or not they want to reestablish residency here.

In response to your program of "earned reentry," the Mennonite Church resolved on September 20, 1974, to "encourage members of our congregations to volunteer as substitutes for those who are required to give a term of work as part of their earned reentry with the commitment that we will work for ways of making this operational."

We are ready to serve as substitutes for these men who acted out of conscience. We make this offer not in the hopes of helping a poor program succeed, but rather to share the unjust burdens of these men who endured exile for their beliefs. Neither do we encourage exiles and deserters to participate in your punitive program, with its implications of wrongdoing, but we affirm the contribution these men of conscience could make to our society if they were allowed to return.

Ideally, we urge you to grant the (unconditional) amnesty these men deserve—to recognize them as the worthwhile citizens they are

---

and not as the criminals your present program implies them to be. Until you realize the wisdom and courage to take this step, we will work in any way possible to help these men return without further hardship and suffering.

As women, who through tradition have not had the chance to voice our opposition to war and violence, we are taking this opportunity to say no to the war machine, no to military aggression, and yes to the young men returning to benefit society.

Beth Sutter, Ruth Sutter, Karen Kreider, Becky Ebersole, Carla Roth, Sandra Mangus, Rhonda Steiner, Susan Herr, Jan Bender, and Dorothy Glanzer, Goshen College, Goshen, IND 46526.[1]

I Had to Review My Life

Michio Ohno, pastor of the Mennonite fellowship in Chiba, Japan, notes that there were fewer than ten known conscientious objectors to war in the whole history of pre-war Japan. Ohno remembers his own pilgrimage of faith, and his conviction regarding peace and reconciliation.

I was among a small group of Christians who met once every two months to study the history and teaching of the sixteenth century Anabaptists. I remember well when a high school student asked Dr. Sakakibara why Anabaptists had been persecuted so much and modern-day Christians were not. The old scholar answered, 'That is because we are not truly Christians.' This shocked me as a thunderbolt. If we act as the people around us do, we will not be persecuted. But then, we may not be faithful to our Lord. I had to review my life if I was worthwhile to be called a Christian, and I was ashamed I was not.

My father being a minister of a Congregational Church, I learned what Japanese churches had done during the war years. There were not many ministers who openly objected to war. They obeyed, reluctantly I hope, to the orders to bow to the direction of the Imperial Palace. They raised money to buy a fighter plane for the army. Members of the church women's fellowships helped to fill 'comfort bags,' and sent them to the soldiers in the front. I knew that we Christians must not make the same mistake again.

When I was serving in the Ashikaga United Church of Christ Church, Tochigi Prefecture, I came to know Ferdinand Ediger, a missionary sent from the General Conference Mennonite Church in America, who helped me to study at the Mennonite Biblical Seminary in Elkhart, Indiana. There I was first exposed to nonresistance and biblical pacifism. There I met people who were willing to sacrifice themselves and practice love. I knew I had finally found the biblical basis of peace movements. After studying two years, I came back to Japan.

In 1972, I began to teach English conversation in small private classes. Two years later, I received a taxable income and I had to file an income tax return for the first time. On the back side of the return form there was a table which showed how our tax money was used for the Japanese military system $(6\frac{1}{2}\%$ in 1973). 'I am a Christian,' I thought. 'I teach people that war is sin, and I pay my money for the preparation of war. It is a self-contradiction.' I filled in the form, but I went to the tax office and told a man in charge that I wanted to refuse paying my income tax until a peaceful use of the tax money was assured, and I returned the statement for payment.

As time went on, a small but growing number of Japanese, including Christians, formed a group called Conscientious Objection to Military Taxes (COMIT). Members of this group withheld a portion of their taxes, according to the percentage of military expenditures in the national budget. Some felt that the payment of war taxes violated their faith. Others felt the Japanese Self Defense Forces, which were supported by the taxes, violated the peace article in the Japanese Constitution.

Law suits were initiated, both to probe the constitutional issues concerned, and to settle the issue of the withheld tax money. In 1988, after eight years of litigation, the Tokyo District Court decided against members of COMIT. In its decision, the court acknowledged that the plaintiffs' feelings based on their faith and conscience were hurt, but stated that the levying and collection of taxes had nothing to do with the rights or freedoms of the group.

I spoke on behalf of the group: "We believe this type of lawsuit, repeated one thousand times, will open the way to legalize conscientious objection to military taxes in Japan."[1]

Making Peace in Vietnam and Nicaragua

Anne Sensenig became acquainted with images of war at a very young age, having grown up in Vietnam during the war. As an adult, Anne's journey took her to Nicaragua with Witness for Peace, where she probed the meaning of her Christian faith among people who suffered from poverty and violence.

I have always been grateful to have been part of a culture other than my birth culture as I grew up. There is something stretching about living in another culture and learning a new language.

U.S. mainstream culture is so powerful and pervasive that only very strong experiences and models can prepare one for alternative ways of life. Growing up in another culture is one such influence which enables one to recognize assumptions and biases that might otherwise remain hidden and unquestioned.

My parents were Eastern Mennonite Board of Missions volunteers in Vietnam from 1963-1973, during the height of U.S. involvement in the Vietnam war. Since I arrived in Vietnam as a two-year-old, I considered my life there to be normal. It was not until I returned to my birth culture that the images from my childhood had the most impact, as I began to realize the striking contrasts between one life and the other.

As a child in Vietnam, I saw and experienced many things: sweet, sticky breakfast rice, wrapped in banana leaves, bought from street vendors whose baskets dangled from shoulder poles; long, hot loaves of French bread; open marketplaces with bright colors, strong smells, people chatting and bargaining, many beggars, often with fingers missing and stumps for legs because of leprosy; playing rubber band jump rope, hopscotch, and jacks (chopsticks and tennis ball) with the neighborhood kids; the hospitality our family experienced, even from the poorest families. I remember feeling bad when we'd go visit poor families, knowing that they would go out and buy a case of soft drinks and ice to serve our family.

There are also images of barbed wire, army trucks, "Military Police" helmets, helicopters, distant gunfire at night, curfews. Once I was awakened by the sound of an explosion, as if in our back yard, and ran to my parents' bedroom for comfort. I found out later that it had been a munitions building six miles away which had been blown up. I remember one day riding to school on the scooter with my dad and sister, and driving through tear gas, apparently in the vicinity of some disturbance in that neighborhood of Saigon. At some point, a Buddhist monk immolated himself in protest of the war at one of the traffic lights I would pass through riding my bike home from school. Hearing about this must have made an impression because I would always think of it when I rode through that intersection.

I can recall, from the third floor of our house, seeing fires from the bombing of a nearby neighborhood where Viet Cong soldiers were suspected to be hiding. That night about sixty refugees who had fled their homes huddled together on the first floor of our house, where English classes were taught during the day.

These images do not fit well into my life in the U.S. I know that at any given moment, somewhere in the world, these kinds of experiences are happening to someone, and the fact that I experienced them has given me a more global understanding of the world.

Though I am a cautious person, it is perhaps not surprising that I ended up spending two years in Nicaragua with Witness for Peace (1986, 1988-1989).

In Nicaragua, I found many similarities to Vietnam—the weather, fruits and vegetables, plants and flowers, open markets, soft drinks, the hospitality of the people and the desire of many to be friends with people of the U.S. despite dislike of our governments' policies. I once again found myself in a country at war—a "civil" war with the U.S. fanning the flames, only this time with a proxy force, the Contras, rather than U.S. troops. Nicaragua was another poor country, struggling to develop, in many ways similar to post-war Vietnam, suffering economically because of a trade and aid embargo by the West, especially the U.S.

Our tasks as volunteers in Nicaragua, included hosting U.S. delegations for two weeks to give them a feel for life in Nicaragua, investigating war-related incidents which affected civilians, and being present, or in solidarity with the Nicaraguans in the war zones, as a gesture of goodwill to counteract the military presence of our government.

I remember on one occasion two of us went to visit Victoriano, a man whose wife and son had been killed the year before when Contras shot into their home. The son, on leave from army duty, was presumably the target of the attack. A younger son had also been wounded by shrapnel. As a result, the family had moved into the larger town of Nueva Guinea in search of safety.

On the day we went to visit Victoriano, we were told that he was at the funeral of another son in the army who had recently been killed. By the time we walked back across town to the church, the burial was over. Victoriano and his now oldest son, also a soldier, were swaying bleary-eyed and drunk by the grave side. They requested we take a picture of the oldest son, as a souvenir in case he too was killed. I walked to their home with the only daughter, eight or nine years old, on whose thin shoulders had fallen the responsibility of taking care of the house, shopping and food preparation, and the care of three younger brothers, an older brother with an injury and her father, unemployed and apparently turned alcoholic. I wonder what the future has held for her, and for that nation of children where one-half the population is under sixteen years old.

On another occasion, two of us accompanied a Mennonite Central Committee volunteer on a visit to a group of Mennonite farmers in the town of La Esperanza in southeastern Nicaragua. They were holding a meeting to discuss ten plots of land they had obtained, on which to grow some food. Their dilemma centered on how to walk the tightrope between the local Sandinista government and the Contras without arousing the suspicion or wrath of either. On the one hand, they were careful not to call their agricultural venture a "co-op" due to fears the Contras would target it as a leftist enterprise. They were not going to own it collectively, and each was to work his own plot. On the other hand, they wanted to walk out to the land together for security, but were afraid the Sandinistas might notice and think they were going out to collaborate with the Contras, as relations between evangelicals and the Sandinistas were not friendly in that area.

My faith was renewed in Nicaragua. Living in a poor country at war sharpened life and death issues. Faith seemed more alive, Christianity seemed to have more relevance to everyday life.

Since my two years in Nicaragua, I trust my government much

less—after seeing the results on the ground of our military support for the Contras. And I am less ready to accept all that I read in newspapers, after living in a country where I could compare what I saw with what I read in U.S. papers. The U.S. journalists in Nicaragua often filed their stories from Managua instead of traveling to the war zones to investigate their stories. Deadlines and the public's fickle interest were what drove them, more than care for thorough investigation. I have also come to distrust any formal political government, no matter what its vision.

One other aspect of my life strengthened by my experiences both in Nicaragua and Vietnam is my conscientious objection to the payment of war taxes (about fifty percent of federal income tax). The stories I've heard and the people I've met have made the issues more clear for me—that I might be paying for the destruction of a friend—and have given me the strength, at least for now, to withhold a portion of my tax as I am able, from the U.S. military arsenals. I am still afraid, and not always certain that this is the best way to go, but when I try to keep the images and experiences before me, the decision is easier.

Master's Degree or CPS Camp?

Delbert Gratz, retired librarian from Bluffton College, OH, reflects on a dilemma he faced in pursuit of his Master's Degree.

During World War II, our local draft board had a stated policy of giving no conscientious objector classifications. All files which indicated such an inclination were turned over to the appeal board. They in turn gave the files to the FBI, who proceeded on a long investigation of each conscientious objector, interviewing neighbors, teachers, and other acquaintances. Finally, they set a day for each person to appear for questioning before a federal judge who had the FBI's inch-thick file of personal information.

As a nervous 22-year-old, I tried to answer the questions the best I could while he made references to my fellow classmates who were dying on some remote Pacific island. Later I was informed by the local draft board that they were directed to give me a 4E classification, and that I would need to report soon for service in a CPS camp. Being in the middle of my last quarter to complete an M.A. degree, I requested that this be postponed by a month, so I could complete my work. Our local representative on the draft board answered that this could be considered if I would agree to be reclassified as IAO (non-combatant work in the army).

I was tempted, because I did want to complete my M.A. work. But for some reason I rather boldly said that I thought the law was the same for the CO as for the non-combatant in regard to deferments. Without an answer I was dismissed, and in two days I had my orders to report to their office for a one-way ticket to CPS Camp #45.

You Are My Children Too

Barbara Ndlovu grew up in Zimbabwe, a country in southern Africa. Born in 1968, she was a child during the struggle for black rule and independence which took place over two decades, 1960-1980. Barbara and her family lived in the area of Tsholotsho, a region which was essentially under the control of the guerilla revolutionary forces.

Barbara's family was deeply involved in the work of the local Brethren in Christ Church. Part of the Anabaptist tradition, Brethren in Christ churches in Zimbabwe were established as a result of North American missionary work. Bishop Stephen Ndlovu notes that the church in Zimbabwe had little understanding of Christ's teaching of love for the enemy as it applied to the war for independence.

Barbara's family and other villagers were sympathetic to the cause of the revolutionary forces, and were frequently subjected to harsh inquiries from government troops. In this context, Barbara remembers her own experiences, and the influence of her grandmother, a leader in the church who displayed courage and dignity under very trying circumstances.

The guerillas were always among the people. They relied on the people for food, clothing—for everything! The people thought that the guerillas were going to save them from the oppressive rule of the white government. They placed a lot of hope in the guerillas.

The government troops lived in camps, but were always out searching for the guerillas and the people who supported them. I remember the day in 1976 when my father was arrested. A short time before his arrest, he had taken a wounded guerilla to the mission hospital for treatment. This was somewhat unusual, since the guerillas normally sought medical treatment in less public places. This news about my father's action apparently reached the government military camp.

On the day of his arrest, my father had driven the church overseer to the city for some business. Upon his return, my father was arrested by soldiers along the road. He was sentenced to five years in prison.

We were all at church when we got the news about my father. I remember I cried a lot that day. His arrest made things very difficult for my family. My mother did not have a job. It was just my mother, grandmother, and the children at home. Some of my uncles who had jobs in the city sent us food and medicines.

At the time of my father's arrest, the school was also closed, because he had been the headmaster. It was a very sad time for me.

During these years, I was scared of white people. The only white people I ever saw were government soldiers, and every time they came to the village they would beat up somebody.

Several weeks after my father's arrest, government soldiers came to our village early in the morning. They surrounded the village. My mother and my aunt were just going out to fetch water for the day, when the soldiers stopped them. They began asking them questions about the guerillas, such as "Where are the guerillas? When did you last see the guerillas? Who is feeding the guerillas? Where did they go?"

My mother tried not to give the soldiers much information, so they began harrassing her. They began to beat my mother in order to force her to give them more information. All we could do was stand and watch, because we were surrounded by soldiers. Finally the soldiers stopped beating my mother, and they went away. Mother was not badly hurt.

We stopped holding worship services in the church because we were afraid the government troops would come and harrass us. Instead we met in my Grandma's house for a short worship service. We prayed together and tried to encourage one another.

I don't remember people in the church talking about Jesus' teaching to love our enemies. We didn't have much time for studying the Bible as a community, since we were afraid to meet for any length of time. It was difficult to think very much about loving the white soldiers. We were always afraid of what they might do to us.

I do remember one Sunday morning, just after the short worship service at Grandma's, the government soldiers came to the village again. Since there had just been a battle between the guerillas and the government soldiers, we were all very fearful. The soldiers surrounded us and began asking the usual questions, "Where are the guerillas? How long ago did they leave? Who fed the guerillas?"

They accused my grandmother of feeding the guerillas and praying with them. My grandmother replied, "They are my children. You are my children too. I will pray with you too if you come to the church."

One of the soldiers began to beat my grandmother, knocking her to the ground. She rose to her feet, and said, "You can only beat me if the Lord Jesus allows you. Let the will of the Lord be done."

He beat her again saying, "The Lord is only for white people."

Once again she rose to her feet and said, "The Lord Jesus forbids you to beat me, so you will not beat me anymore." The other soldiers ordered him to stop, and they left the village.

Many things improved with the coming of independence and peace in 1980. My father was released from prison, after having been there for four years. We had a new black government, and there were no more white soldiers coming to our village to harm us.

I Am an Evangelist, I Cannot Kill a Man

Themba Nkawu was the first Brethren in Christ young man to refuse military service in Zimbabwe. Themba and Bishop Ndlovu (of the Zimbabwe Brethren in Christ Church) relate the story:

Bishop Ndlovu calls Themba a "God-fearing dynamic man prepared to do his work. He was a student in the Bible School, where he studied the Bible, as well as Brethren in Christ life and thought.

"During the revolution, the government instituted conscription, which put tremendous pressure on our young people," says Bishop Ndlovu. "The army came to people's homes, without advance warning, to take young people for military training. As a church, we were not prepared for this. Many of our youth had not been taught to apply Christ's command to love our enemies to situations of warfare.

"Our youth had very difficult choices before them. If they were picked up by the military, they would be forced to fight against their own brothers in the forest. If they fled to the forest, they might be forced to join the guerrillas. Our own son, for example, fled to the countryside to live with his cousin in order to escape military conscription. He didn't even tell us that he was planning to leave. We were very worried about him because he just disappeared. Only a month later did we find out that he was safe.

"Themba Nkawu had graduated from Bible School and was preaching freely, when he was conscripted by the military. Themba went through basic training, but then said, 'I am an evangelist. I cannot kill a man.' At that point, he was taken away from his unit, and we did not know what had happened to him. We all feared that he had been killed, but as it turned out, he was simply held under arrest. Perhaps a week later, Themba was released."

"I was released on condition that if I was caught addressing a

---

political meeting, I would be arrested again," recalls Themba. "This is what they thought I was doing. But I was released because I had said I was a preacher, so they did not force me to do what I did not want to do."

According to Bishop Ndlovu, Themba continued to preach fearlessly upon his release. Themba notes, however, that this was not without difficulty. "Sometimes I was asked to send my preaching schedule to the Central Police Station. After that, I noticed that some members of the police force attended the gatherings in which I preached."

From the Flying Club to Civilian Public Service

T he year was 1940, and life was going well for Clyde Mosemann. At the age of twenty, he was already enjoying the fruits of economic success. "I had a new two-toned convertible," recalls Clyde. "Some of us formed a flying club and bought a plane. I soloed and took a course at Franklin and Marshall College for my private license. The club grew and we bought a second plane."

Clyde owed his success to his good job as foreman of the carving department at Sensenich Brothers, a manufacturer of airplane propellers. "I was making 70 dollars per week, very good wages in those times," he remembers. "The average wage of a common laborer was 15 to 20 dollars per week." It was an exciting time to enter the job market. Wages were on the increase, and American industry was gearing up for military production as World War II loomed ever closer on the horizon.

It was not long, however, until Clyde began having serious doubts about his employment. The world at war had come to Clyde's carving bench in the form of a contract to manufacture propellers for U.S. Army trainer aircraft. This troubled Clyde's conscience. "Christ taught us the way of peace," he says. "Christ's kingdom is not of this world. He taught us to love our enemies. I had developed firm convictions about this from the time I was a boy at East Chestnut Street Mennonite Church. I felt uncomfortable accepting wages earned from production which was going for war purposes."

Conversations with other Mennonite employees at Sensenich Brothers did not all yield the same concern. "A top member of the management team and a staunch Mennonite downplayed the situation, reminding me that we didn't make propellers for combat planes. He said that I was making good wages, that I would be receiving promotions as the company grew, and that I would probably be deferred by the draft board."

When the Japanese attacked Pearl Harbor and the U.S. joined the war, however, Clyde and fellow employee Roy Bucher decided that they could no longer work at their jobs with a clear conscience. So in December of 1941, they quit their jobs and went to Florida.

The decision radically changed the direction of Clyde's life. He soon found employment with Stokeley Canning Company. Although the 15-dollar-a-week salary was barely adequate, Clyde never questioned his decision. He began working at the Spanish Mennonite Mission in Ybor City, an experience which helped him understand the needs of the broader society.

Upon his return from Florida in the Spring, Clyde found a letter from the local draft board which classified him as 1AO, eligible for noncombatant service in the military. Clyde appealed. As a conscientious objector to war, he wished to perform alternate service under the provisions of the Burke-Wadsworth Act.[1]

Over the course of the next several months, Clyde appealed the ruling several times until the case reached Federal Court. The FBI became involved, visiting his girlfriend and others who knew Clyde. They questioned Clyde's associates about his beliefs, his moral life and church affiliation. On June 17, 1942, Clyde was ordered to appear in Federal Court in Philadelphia to testify once again to his beliefs as a conscientious objector.

"The officer questioned me concerning my beliefs and the beliefs of my church," remembers Clyde. "He then began a tirade of verbal abuse, accusing me of being a traitor to my country in time of need, and of being a coward. I paused, and looked out the window (we were on the fifth or sixth floor) at a statue of William Penn on top of the building next to us and said, 'Sir, was William Penn a coward and a traitor to his country?' He stuttered around a bit and then with a much more congenial attitude noted that Quakers were 'good people.'"

In several weeks, Clyde was reclassified 4E, conscientious objector. What followed was a series of assignments in Civilian Public Service Camps. There his work included forestry, as well as assignments in mental hospitals, until his release on May 17, 1946.

When he was released, Clyde enrolled in college, then attended seminary. In 1953, he began serving his church as a missionary in South America. Even there, Clyde's commitment to Christ's way of peace was not without controversy. "I preached a sermon on peace in the church in Buenos Aires, and received a great deal of negative reaction. The members felt there was a great danger that if the military heard of our peace position they would close our church. In those days, there was a great deal of violence between the military factions."

Clyde notes the impact which his initial choice to leave his job has had on his life. "In being obedient to God, He has blessed me in many ways and has opened a greater and fuller life for me. During my CPS service, I learned about our great Anabaptist history and vision, and began to feel a call from God as I was more and more exposed to the needs of a hurting world."

A Toolmaker's Dilemma

A fellow employee said registrant lives a good clean life and has never heard him use a curse word. He said registrant has mentioned to him his stand against the use of force and against military service, and has stated that he would not sit on a jury of a trial involving an offense in which capital punishment may be the penalty.
　　　　　—From an FBI inquiry into the life of David Pierantoni dated May 23, 1958

D avid Pierantoni is a Mennonite man who has struggled with the meaning of his commitment to Christ's way of peace for over thirty years. As a youth, the issue was military service and an unyielding draft board. As an adult, the problem was military-related employment and an unsympathetic employer.

In 1955 David Pierantoni turned eighteen years old and was required to register with his local draft board in New York City. David chose to register as a conscientious objector.

Unknown to David at the time, this was the beginning of a long odyssey of appeals, court appearances and FBI checks on his background and character. Following an unsuccessful attempt to have his classification changed to that of a conscientious objector, David decided to appeal to President Eisenhower. In a letter to President Eisenhower dated February 13, 1960, David wrote:

"Please do not feel that I am trying to be disloyal to my country. The Bible does teach Christians to be submissive to government, but when the government requests something contrary to God's word which teaches us to love one another, we must be loyal to God first.

"There was a time in my life, even since I made my claim, that I was going to join the Navy just to be with my brother. But after careful consideration, I found that I could not remain loyal to my

---

church, my convictions and especially my God. It is my duty to apply God's word to my life daily."

During the next five years, the FBI frequently contacted David's employer and neighbors, trying to assess whether David's character and life were consistent with that of a conscientious objector. Despite a positive report from the FBI, the local draft board rejected David's request for classification as a conscientious objector. Instead, he was granted a family deferment.

In more recent years, David's conscience against war was tested in new ways. David was offered a job at Hamilton Technology in Lancaster, Pennsylvania, as a toolmaker. He declined the job because of the company's production of military weaponry, such as fuzes and primers for bombs and artillery shells.

In 1984 David was stricken with a case of arthritis and tendonitis, which became severe in the winter months. He began to look for job opportunities in a warmer climate, where his arthritis would be less of a problem.

During a visit with his daughter in Florida, David was offered a job at a local tool shop. "While touring the facility, I noticed some injection mold systems which were used to produce detonators for bombs and grenades. When I asked the owner about these operations, he declined to discuss them since they were part of a government contract which would soon be terminated."

David did not pursue this employment opportunity further during his visit to Florida. Several weeks later, however, the owner of the company called David at his home in Pennsylvania, asking if he would consider moving to Florida, since the company was in need of another toolmaker. "I told Mr. Wilson* that I could not in clear conscience design parts which would be used in the production of military weapons. He assured me that this contract was nearly terminated and, that by the time I moved to Florida, it would be completed."

Over the next several weeks, David held additional phone conversations with the owner of Perfection Tool and Mold Company. The owner assured David that no military work would be involved in his assignment.

David saw this opportunity as a good way to accommodate his health needs, and the family moved to Florida.

A few days after David began working at Perfection Tool and Die,

*Fictitious name

he became aware of a section of the building which was closed off to others. Several weeks later he noticed that some personnel entered the plant, used the time clock, and then entered the closed off section. David began hearing the sounds of an injection mold machine in production.

One day David noticed that the door to the closed-off section was left open during a lunch break. Curiosity got the best of David, and he wandered inside to find trays of detonator parts for grenades.

"When I asked Mr. Wilson about the detonator parts, he told me that this work was being done by a separate department, complete with its own management and personnel. He said the use of the time clock was merely a matter of courtesy included in the lease.

"Five weeks after beginning my employment, I was handed some blueprints for a priority job. When I noticed that the blueprints were for parts for an injection mold machine, I remembered that I had not heard the machine running that day. I told my supervisor that I had an understanding with Mr. Wilson that I would not do military-related work. When Mr. Wilson arrived on the scene, he asked me what the problem was, grabbed the prints, and told me that I was being stubborn.

"Two weeks before Christmas I was given a temporary lay-off, due to a lack of work. Several days later though, he called me in for a chat. He told me that the future workload looked very promising and included lucrative bonuses. The work, however, was all government contracts with military specifications. I reminded Mr. Wilson of my strong convictions against doing military work. Mr. Wilson replied that in that case, he could no longer use me as an employee."

David was unemployed for four and a half months. At the end of February, his former employer in Pennsylvania offered to hire David again. The family made plans to move back to Pennsylvania. While loading their U-Haul, however, he received a call from another Florida employer which manufactured pharmaceutical packaging machinery. David took the job and remained in Florida.

In retrospect David says that it appears that Mr. Wilson misled him from the very beginning. "I have at times resented the experience," says David, "but I'm sure I can live with it peaceably."

Summing up his experiences as a conscientious objector, David notes, "As I see our world of conflict and war, I take the consolation of knowing my contribution to my fellow man is of a constructive nature and not a destructive one."

Dedicated to God

*R. S. Lemuel, son of Mennonite Brethren ministers from Manabub-
nager, India, and member of the International Mennonite Peace
Committee, reflects on his decision not to pursue a career in the Navy.*

I did not have any special attraction to the Navy. But for the
sake of a job, and because I had good academic grades, I went
with a friend to the Navy office for an interview when I was
eighteen years old. Military service in India is not compulsory but
young people choose it because there are few other employment
options. Military pay is better than for most other jobs and children
of military personnel receive special educational and employment
benefits. I felt additional pressure to get a good, secure job because
I was the eldest son in the family. Being the eldest in India means
working hard to care for the remaining family members.

"Once at the Navy office, however, I could not go through with the
interview. I had a strong inner struggle not to join the Navy and
returned home without taking any of the necessary tests. I was
especially influenced by missionary John A. Wiebe, my pastor J.
John, and my parents. Rev. J. John taught us not even to join the
police force. The Bible has also been a strong resource for me in my
peace position, especially Jesus' Sermon on the Mount in Matthew
five. In addition, I had been recognized as having leadership gifts
in solving local disputes within my own age group. With all of this
background, I was able to refrain from pursuing the Navy interview,
even though I was tempted by the job."

Eventually, Lemuel went on to seminary studies and church
work. The path was not an easy one however. As Lemuel now sees
it, his decision to go to seminary was finally an "answer to the
prayers of my parents, who were the village preachers. Before my
birth they named me Lemuel, which means 'dedicated to God.' Even
though I was the oldest child, they hoped that I would become a
full-time minister of the Gospel. Although the initial call was in my

heart, I did not respond immediately. Instead, I took a civil engineering degree to get a good government job. That did not work. Later on I took a lab technician course and began to work in our Mennonite Brethren Medical Centre in Jadcherla. While serving in that hospital, God spoke to me in many ways to change my mind, even using bitter experiences such as accidents and ill health in my family. Finally, I earnestly prayed to God to show me the right direction. Then God specifically spoke to me from Luke 12:47: 'That slave who knew what his master wanted, but did not prepare himself or do what was wanted, will receive a severe beating.' After consulting a missionary friend, I decided to go to seminary."

Lemuel now counsels other young men who face dilemmas similar to the one he once faced. One young man who came to him had found employment with the army as an electrical engineer. Two years into his career, however, he was asked to learn the Russian language in order to help manufacture special lenses for missiles. With Lemuel's assistance, he was able to explain the faith and practice of the Mennonite Church, and secure transfer to another department.[1]

The Lesson is to Always Trust God

Allen Stuckey, a medical doctor, went to Vietnam in September of 1969 as a Mennonite Central Committee (MCC) worker. While there, Allen had a life-threatening experience which continues to affect his life and faith today.

I went to Vietnam believing that military service was not an option for me, but that my pacifist religious beliefs should not be used as an easy escape from the draft," says Allen. "Many young men of my age were being drafted into military service where they frequently had to face physical and psychological trauma, as well as death in combat. It did not seem fair to me, or even responsible to my belief in pacifism, to choose to do alternate service in a church-sponsored service program in a country other than Vietnam."

Allen credits his congregation for his commitment to service. "Early in childhood, we were influenced by the missionary emphasis in our church, especially the stories of missionary workers. These stories were further reinforced by the experiences of young men who had gone into PAX service after World War II, and family experiences with Civilian Public Service." The death of Dr. Paul Carlson (missionary in the Congo), and the abduction of Daniel Gerber (MCC worker in Vietnam) led Allen to a personal commitment to go to Vietnam if the war continued beyond the completion of his medical internship in July of 1969. In September of that year, Allen, his wife Jeannie, and son Jonathan volunteered to work in Vietnam, and began a three-year term of service.

Perhaps at no time during his work in Vietnam was Allen's faith more severely tested or immeasurably strengthened, than during an experience in the town of Pleiku.

The story of this experience begins in the examination room of the Vietnam Christian Service (VNCS) hospital in the town of Pleiku. Each morning, Allen worked with a Vietnamese interpreter and received Vietnamese patients. In the afternoons, there was a walk-in clinic for the tribal people.

Allen was examining a young tribal boy on Good Friday afternoon in April of 1971, when the door to the examining room was pushed open by a South Vietnamese military officer. At the time, Allen was unaware that the officer was the commander of the military base just across the road from the hospital. The commander's presence in the room meant that he had already used his considerable authority to bypass the routine procedures for requesting medical treatment at the hospital. Speaking through the interpreter, the commander demanded that his two little boys, who were ill, be examined immediately. Allen patiently tried to explain that he needed to see the tribal patients first, but that he would be happy to examine the commander's sons later that afternoon.

The commander continued to speak to the interpreter, making it very difficult for Allen to listen to the chest of his patient, whom he feared might have tuberculosis. Finally, Allen stood, placed his hand on the commander's shoulder, and said as politely as he could in Vietnamese, "Please excuse me, sir. I need to examine this child. Please leave."

The commander left, and by the end of the day, Allen had forgotten about the incident. That evening, Allen went home to the VNCS house, located just up the hill from the hospital, to share a casual evening meal with his family and other expatriates who worked at the hospital and in the community.

"We had spent about an hour eating, and one of the young men who had been there for several years was telling us about Viet Cong (South Vietnamese revolutionaries who were fighting against the government, and were supported by North Vietnam) atrocities and Viet Cong attacks. It was unreal how we had just finished talking about that, when the door flew open and a man, whom we will call Officer Lo, came into the room and said, 'Where is Dr. Stuckey?' I told him a couple of times that I was Dr. Stuckey, but since I didn't look like a physician in my shirt and sandals, he seemed to think we were up to something. Bill, the most experienced worker with us, immediately stood up and said, 'Get some tea for this man,' and encouraged him to sit down between us.

"I noticed that Officer Lo had a shoulder pistol, that the flap was open, and that the gun was ready to fire. Something was obviously very wrong. We spent a whole half hour gradually helping Officer Lo feel comfortable. He wanted me to go with him to his house in Pleiku, because his wife had prepared a banquet meal in appreciation for my treatment of his sons earlier that week. Officer Lo was not the man that I had seen in the clinic earlier that day, and I did not connect the two events for the following forty-five minutes.

"During the course of our conversation, which was really a very pleasant one, he told us that he had been to a U.S. military base for training, and had had some very unpleasant experiences. Suddenly he turned, stared at me and said, 'You're like all the other Americans. You think Americans are intelligent, and Vietnamese are dumb.' His intensity really bothered both Bill and myself. It was clear that he was referring to something other than this situation. I replied, 'No, I don't speak Vietnamese very well. You speak English very well, and I enjoy talking to Vietnamese who can speak English as well as you can.'

"After I declined his third invitation to go to his home, he stood up, drew his pistol, and told us all to remain seated. He then started yelling at the top of his voice for two other men to come. A young man came in with his M-16 (machine gun), followed by a fifteen or sixteen-year-old boy who also carried an M-16. The men situated themselves in other sections of the room, obviously assuming that we had weapons, and that there was potential for a gun battle.

"After asking again which one was Dr. Stuckey (they still seemed distrustful of my answer), one of the men grabbed me by the nape of the neck and pulled me up to take me out to a jeep which was waiting in our lane. I told him that there was no need to be forceful, and that I would go with them.

"At this point, both Bill and I were fairly sure that this was the prelude to an attack by the Viet Cong. In a similar situation in the past, and also twelve days later in Di Linh, the Viet Cong had used a VNCS house as a barricade from which to attack a South Vietnamese military base. The other possibility was that these were Viet Cong dressed in South Vietnamese uniforms. They probably needed a doctor to take care of some wounded comrades, so they had come for me to help them.

"I had every hope that I would be returning unharmed, after having given them medical services. As far as I was concerned, it was all up to me.

"As I was telling the officer that there was no need to be forceful, he hit me over the head with his pistol, and I decided again that I had to be as cooperative as possible.

"Despite my best efforts at stalling for time while appearing to be cooperative, I did finally get into the jeep. I sat in the front with the officer, while the two armed youth were joined in the back seat by a third soldier who had been guarding the outside of the house. My captors were nervous, and the jeep left the MCC house at a high rate of speed. A short distance down the road, one of the M-16s in the back seat fired through the canvas roof of the jeep. This put everyone even more on edge.

"As we drove along I turned to the colonel and tried to tell him that I would cooperate, that they could put the guns away. I got as far as the word 'cooperate' when the officer slapped me across the cheek.

"At that moment, on the glove compartment door of the jeep, I saw a clear vision of the face of Christ with the crown of thorns and the blood running down his forehead. Off to the left of that was a lamb, and along the bottom it seemed like I could see the words to Isaiah 53:7:

He was oppressed, and he was afflicted, yet he opened not his mouth; he is brought as a lamb to the slaughter, and as a sheep before her shearers is dumb, so he openeth not his mouth.

"A distinct change came over me—from a person who was still trying to control the situation, I became one who was willing to submit to whatever was going to happen.

"By now it was dark. The jeep passed under a large gateway, then turned down a long gravel lane. We were in the Buddhist cemetery. I could see the headlights shining on all the tombstones. I thought, 'This is where the Viet Cong often have tunnels.' Most of the Vietnamese stay away from cemeteries because they revere their ancestors. So I began to wonder which one of these big gravestones concealed the opening to a tunnel, and what it would be like inside.

"One of the soldiers in the back seat grabbed me around the neck and pulled me up over the seat. Together with one of his partners, he put me under the back seat. It was an open seat that you could flip up, so I was in a box-like enclosure. One of them continued to keep a choke-hold on my neck. I could not understand what was going on, but it seemed like I was told to just relax and let God take care of me. My medical, or more rational side, thought perhaps they wanted me to become unconscious. I decided to speed up the process and act totally unconscious.

"Next they put a handkerchief in my mouth, bound my hands and removed my watch. They grabbed me by the feet, and pulled me out of the jeep, over the bumper, and onto the gravel. I had decided to remain as still and limp as possible, but I did curl up to protect myself as I was being pulled.

"After this, I was ordered to sit up. I ended up in a kneeling position with my hands bound and a gag in my mouth. The officer pulled his gun and placed it on my forehead. At that point I knew this was terribly different from what I had expected. The officer began a long harangue about the fact that I was an American guest. I felt his deep-seated hatred for Americans. In many ways, I understood this hatred directed at the foreigners who were occupying his country.

"He told me that he was there to kill me. He said he needed to kill me for insulting his commanding officer by not seeing his sons that afternoon. When he asked if I remembered seeing his commander's sons, I literally could not remember what he was talking about (I hadn't actually seen the sons), so I shook my head 'No.' This enraged the officer, and he ordered the other men to kick me down.

"He again had me sit up in the same position and started over with the same message, getting more and more angry. He went through his whole speech again about how I as an American guest in his country thought I was better than everyone else. When he again asked me about the commander's sons, I nodded my head 'Yes,' indicating that I did recall the commander's request. Again, he kicked me down, and I wondered if this was my last reprieve.

"He got me up a third time. As the muzzle of the gun came to my forehead, all I could think was, 'I don't believe I am going to hear anything. This is going to be a very quick death.' But this time, after he had gone through his speech he said, 'If I spare your life you must promise that you will never tell what has happened to you. If you tell, I will find you, and kill you or have you killed.' I agreed, of course. After going over this several times, he kicked me down again. Then they all got into the jeep, backed down the driveway, and sped off through the archway.

"I lay motionless, not willing to trust that the ordeal was over. Finally, I sat up and looked up into the sky. There I saw a beautiful moon, and a tremendous sense of peace came over me. I didn't know for sure what lay ahead, but I knew that God had protected me so far. I sensed very strongly that somebody I knew had known that I was in deep trouble. It was almost like I could see my father's face in the sky, as well as another face, perhaps of my sister Orlene.

"About a year and a half later I discovered that my father had indeed known that I was in trouble. He had gone up to the hay mow on Good Friday morning (Eastern Daylight Time in Ohio is thirteen hours behind Vietnam) to throw hay down for the steers. As he was taking a bale of hay to throw down into the hayrack, he suddenly had an intense feeling that I was in a great deal of danger. Instead of throwing the bale down the hole, he put it on the floor and knelt right there to pray for me. After praying for a while, he felt a remarkable peace and sensed that I was going to be okay.

"More recently my aunt, whose facial features are very similar to my sister's, told me a similar story. She was vacuuming the house that Good Friday morning when she somehow knew that I was in trouble. She too stopped to kneel down and pray for me. I am convinced that these prayers were the real factors which altered the course of events for me.

"There in the graveyard, I took in this strong sense of God's presence, and suddenly realized that I had to return to the hospital as quickly as possible. I had agreed not to tell anyone what had happened, but my family and my colleagues back at the house were probably already reporting my abduction.

"With considerable fear, I left the cemetery and headed down the street toward Pleiku. I hadn't gone far until I came upon a small village. The dogs began to bark and the children came running. There was no way I could avoid a crowd. I was taken to the village elder's house, where I was treated very kindly. I was anxious about getting back to the hospital, and asked repeatedly if someone could take me. The villagers, however, wanted to treat my wounds and find out what had happened to me. Finally the village elder indicated that arrangements had been made to give me a ride to the hospital. Much to my dismay, the one who came to my aid was a South Vietnamese soldier on a Honda with an M-16 slung over his shoulder! Perhaps God was teaching me that Good Samaritans may come in many guises.

"The incident passed, and I survived. Yet something happened that Easter Sunday which gave the experience special meaning, and guaranteed its continuing influence on my life. On Easter Sunday morning, I woke up very early, and went outside to read my Bible and pray. Once again I felt a wonderful sense of peace and the nearness of God. I decided to go to the tribal church in Pleiku knowing that I would hardly understand a word.

"Throughout the service, I felt a tremendous sense of God's power, and the presence of the Holy Spirit. I felt a strange feeling in my throat, and I began to wonder about the gift of speaking in tongues. I dismissed the thought quickly.

"I was not particularly interested in that gift, and for nine years after that Easter Sunday in 1971, I denied that it was there. It wasn't until Easter weekend in Boston in 1980 that I allowed it to happen. I had been feeling quite low in spirit, and was recalling again the events of that Easter weekend in Vietnam. There in the hospital in Boston, I allowed myself to speak in tongues. Nobody has heard me speak in tongues since, and I don't have any plans to use the gift publicly. For me, it is a prayer language. I really believe that God gave this gift to me because he knew that I was one of those Christians who needed that kind of spiritual encouragement and strengthening.

"This experience has changed my life. Before this, I was intellectually guarded about the power of prayer. Through this 'prayer language' I am convinced that prayer is our way of communicating with our creator. It has taught me to not try to take charge of things, but to let the hand of God lead me. When I do that, things happen more efficiently, and so much more to the glory of God.

"I was in Pleiku for one very difficult week after the incident. I found it very hard to sleep. But I continued to feel a strong sense of God's presence and knew that ultimately I had nothing to worry about. I did not even think of arming myself, and I continued to sleep in my bed right beside the window. At the end of the week, I returned to my work at the hospital in Nha Trang.

"Just twelve days after this happened to me, Ted Studebaker, a Church of the Brethren worker with Vietnam Christian Service, was killed during a Viet Cong attack in the village of Di Linh. Ted was a man of peace, and someone we had all grown to love and appreciate. When I heard of Ted's death, I felt guilty for having survived my ordeal. I also wondered why God had failed to provide protection for Ted, when God had protected me. It seemed paradoxical. For Christians, however, I believe the lesson is always to trust God for protection, rather than relying on one's own strength or weapons for defense. This commitment to the way of peace is important for my walk with God now. In the long run, eternal life with God is more important than defending oneself in this life. God used Ted's witness in a very significant way. The letters and tapes which he had sent home communicated the Gospel of peace even in the midst of a tragic situation.

"About six to eight weeks after the incident in Pleiku, a Vietnamese investigator came to talk with me about what had happened, and I made a very general statement. I told him that I did not want anyone to be prosecuted. I knew there were many Vietnamese who had been killed or unjustly treated by Americans, without any hope of a trial or restitution."

As Allen reflects on his experience in Vietnam, he notes that, "the experience of death and resurrection as celebrated each Easter season has become a period of annual revitalization for all aspects of my life.

"Having met the Prince of Peace in a life-changing way in the midst of a tragic civil war has meant that subsequent life struggles have been manageable, and that beneath those struggles is always the assurance of peace, faith, and hope."

Choosing Separation

During the American Civil War, in the spring of 1862, Henry G. Brunk decided to flee to the North to escape induction into the Southern army. Shortly after his marriage to Susanna Heatwole, he joined a group of some 70 Mennonite and Brethren men and boys who were setting out for Ohio. The accounts of Mennonite historian J. C. Wenger and Henry G. Brunk's granddaughter, Ethel Estella Erb, form the basis of this story.

Shortly after passing through Petersburg, West Virginia, the group was stopped by two Confederate Scouts and told to surrender their arms. They offered their Bibles and Testaments but were told they could keep them. The Confederates marched them on foot on the long and wearisome route through Franklin and Monterey to Staunton. There they were put on a train and transported to a Richmond prison, where they remained for about six weeks.

The prisoners were then given their choice of putting on the uniform and taking up arms, hauling provisions (noncombatant work) or being prisoners. They chose noncombatant work, because noncombatants were not required to put on uniforms and their duties included care of the sick in the army and hauling hay from the large bank barns for the cavalry horses.

Henry believed at first that he could do noncombatant work, but after a time, he felt that after all, it was a part of the machinery for the destruction of men. So one day, while waiting his turn to get his load in the barn, he left the team he had in charge and strolled through the big orchard and timbers to his home in Harrisonburg. From that time he was considered a deserter with a price on his head, and he would have been killed if found. His friends and neighbors helped to conceal him, and he lived in hiding, here and there, often in their garrets, for two and a half years. Sometimes he made willow whip baskets. Neighbors' children would tell him quietly, if they saw a soldier coming.

Meanwhile at home, Henry's wife Susanna had borne their second child. At the end of his first year of hiding, their son, little John Albert, died. Susanna stood alone at the grave. From the edges of the crowd, Henry watched as an anonymous stranger until the last hymn was sung and the tiny grave was being filled. Then he hurried away, for the army scouts were there, expecting to find him among the mourners.

One day he was confronted on the road by a neighbor on horseback who had been sent by the Confederate Army to find him and bring him in. The neighbor knew him well but failed to recognize him. He asked Henry if he knew anyone who could tell him the whereabouts of Henry G. Brunk. Henry told him to ask at a house a half mile to the west. As the neighbor galloped off on his horse, Henry hurried to his hiding place.

The hiding grew more and more perilous. Henry decided to try once more to escape to the North. He joined a group of seventeen, most of them still quite young. They met at Weavers Mennonite Church at midnight and made their way to Rawley Springs. At first they traveled only at night. Later they hired two guides to lead them toward the freedom of the North. As much as possible, they stayed in the mountains. Sometimes they could see the campfires of the soldiers in the valleys below. They finally arrived in Hagerstown, Maryland, where Henry found employment in a leather shop, mending shoes and harnesses.

When Henry and Susanna had last seen each other, he had told her to come to Maryland after the war, so that they could try to find each other. Susanna waited, but no word came. She could not bear the suspense and uncertainty. She determined to take her baby by horse and spring wagon and try to follow out between the armies as the Union Army fell back to the North, followed by the Rebels.

Susanna was shy and timid by nature, but when Confederate Soldiers grabbed her horse's bridle to take the horse, Susanna clung to the reins and said firmly, "You will do no such thing!" At that moment voices yelled, "The Yanks are coming," and the soldiers ran, leaving the horse to Susanna.

At Harpers Ferry, the bridge was burning and she was too late to cross it. A miller told her where and how some people drove across the river. Nothing could daunt her. She held the baby tight and plunged in.

At last she drove into Hagerstown, a stranger, still having no word

---

of whether her husband was living or dead. She stopped in the street and did not know what to do or where to go. She looked at the faces of all who passed by but could not hope to see him. She looked through the window of a store front—and there she saw him at a shoemaker's bench making shoes!

It was a glorious reunion for both.[1]

I Have Lived through Five Wars

Henry Fast (deceased) and his wife Ethel, Mennonites from Kansas, were over eighty years old when they began withholding war taxes. Excerpts from two of their letters to the IRS (Internal Revenue Service) appear below.

1985
Box 125
North Newton, KS 67117

Internal Revenue Service
Austin, Texas

Dear Sir:

In World War I, I was a conscientious objector to war, and I so reported to the military camp informing them I could not participate in regular military training. But I asked to be assigned to service in a "Base Hospital for Overseas Patients." They respected my claim of conscience, so I helped to serve many "face" and "stomach" victims of war. Later upon my discharge from service they handed me an "honorable discharge" card (I still have it). Can you grant this kind of courtesy now to a 90-year-old man and his spouse of 85 and indicate a similar sensitive concern for a claim of conscience I am going to lay before you?

We love our country, "one nation under God." To us this really implies that all nations exist only by the grace of God. We respect our government and do not hesitate to pay taxes for orderly affairs and services of government.

But we have become deeply troubled over the large proportion of our federal income tax that is used to build up our growing military armaments and arsenal at the expense of the poor, the sick, the aged, the unemployed. Our conscience cannot endure this, so we have decided to withhold 36.8% of our federal tax liability, that is, the percentage used in the present military build-up program, and send this as a donation to the Commission of Home Ministries of the General Conference of the Mennonite Church. The work of this commission I know personally from close contact. "Home Ministries" limits this service to our own country. And its service reaches out to the poor, the unemployed in overcrowded cities and to groups from Third World peoples--Hispanics, Chinese, etc.--in order to help them get on their feet, feel at home in strange places, handle discriminations and handicaps, find a sense of self-importance and learn the art of community living in our country."

Can you grant us this kind of courtesy for our older years of 90 and 85 and allow this offer as acceptable in spirit in the given situation? And truly a "Thank you."

Check for $1,161.00 is enclosed
Check for $675.00 to Commission for Home Ministries has been forwarded
Total Tax liability $1,836.00

Signed,
Henry A. Fast
Ethel S. Fast

◆

April 5, 1988
Box 125
North Newton KS 67117

Regional Director
Internal Revenue Service
Austin, TX 73301

Dear Director,
As the tax deadline approaches, I am again faced with the troubling knowledge of where my tax dollars are going. I would like to make the following comments.

I am 93 years old and my wife is 88. I have lived through five wars and have seen the destruction of life and spirit that results. I have been deeply troubled over the disproportionate amount of federal income taxes which are used for building up a vast over-supply of military arms and armaments.

I have been a conscientious objector to war and the military all of my life. In this country people now are able to exercise their consciences and not participate physically in military service. But there are many of us who are also conscientious objectors to paying for military protection and service.

I have been a supporter of legislation that would provide an acceptable alternative for people who want to pay all their income taxes, but do not want to pay for military build-up. If the Peace Tax Fund legislation became law, my wife and I could happily pay all our taxes in good conscience, knowing that instead of going for military preparations, our taxes would be used for peaceful causes.

As I have been a taxpayer for a good many years, I hope you will respect my wishes in this matter. Older and faithful taxpayers shouldn't be harassed with computer letters and threatened with penalties. Perhaps instead of threatening people who want to pay all their taxes but don't want those taxes used for military build-up, the Internal Revenue Service should encourage Congress to pass the Peace Tax Fund bill! I am enclosing a brochure for your information.

Sincerely,
Henry A. Fast
Ethel S. Fast

I Could Have Killed My Cousin!

In 1945, a German Mennonite named Siegfried Bartel emerged from World War II, having served as a Captain in the German Army. Today, Siegfried talks to Mennonite youth about the centrality of peace and reconciliation in the teachings of Christ. Siegfried's story is one of obedience, defeat, and transformation.

Siegfried's mother kept a diary in the year preceding his birth (1914). The diary reveals prayers that the German emperor and soldiers would be granted victory. In Siegfried's youth, he remembers hearing little criticism of the government or of Hitler. He heard little from the church about issues of war and peace.

Hitler was enormously popular when elected in 1933. Hitler worked wonders with the devastated rural economy. He restructured farm debts and made certain that no farmers were forced to leave their land due to the economic crisis. Most of the German Mennonites were farmers and, along with many others, viewed Hitler as an economic savior for Germany.

On September 10, 1933, the Conference of West Prussian Mennonites in Tiegenhagen, sent a telegram to Hitler, stating, "The conference realizes with deep gratitude the tremendous upheaval, which God gave to our people with your energy," and vowed on their part, "cheerful cooperation for the reconstruction of our Fatherland out of the strengths of the gospel." Hitler in return thanked them for their "true spirit and readiness to cooperate."

The conservative Mennonites in South Germany were more reluctant to react and remained silent.[1]

"Mennonites in Germany had officially dropped the nonresistant position after World War I," says Siegfried. "All the young men I knew served in the army—Mennonites as well as others. It was not

---

a problem for me because everyone else was serving—we saw it as our duty. As a Christian, I didn't even consider not serving. We had accepted the Lutheran teaching of the 'two kingdoms.'"

Siegfried's father-in-law, Emil Siebert, was the only German Mennonite Siegfried knew who had any reservations about Hitler. He expressed his reservations in his sermons, using Old Testament texts to refer to Hitler's misuse of power. Out of consideration for Emil Siebert's safety, the local Ministerial Council, under the leadership of elder Cornelius Dirksen, did not allow him to continue preaching.

In this context, Siegfried volunteered in the army in 1937. He fully intended to serve for two years and then return to farming.

In September of 1939, however, at the beginning of World War II, Siegfried's unit joined in an effort to unite Germany by attacking the Polish army. According to Siegfried, the "need" for this action went back to the Versailles Treaty at the end of World War I. German-speaking people were divided by a corridor of land which gave Poland access to the sea. From the start of the war, Siegfried and others assumed that this was the only objective. After a quick military strike through the corridor, Germany would be unified, and the war would be over.

On the first day of the war, Siegfried's unit was ordered to storm a hill in the Polish corridor. "We got into the area where my father was born," he explains, "and where most of his relatives were living. They lived within twenty kilometers of the hill. Many of our close relatives thought it would be wonderful to come back into the German family."

Siegfried directed his unit to pepper the hill with fifteen-centimeter grenades. In the aftermath of the battle, Siegfried and his fellow soldiers walked to the top of the hill. On the slope, Siegfried found a wounded enemy soldier who had been bandaged and left behind by his compatriots. "Are you Polish?" Siegfried asked. The soldier replied in perfect German, "No, I am a Lutheran."

The soldier was one of many Germans living in the Polish corridor who had been recruited by the Polish military. Siegfried's first thought was, "Man, I could have killed my cousin!" He remembered a cousin, Walter Schroeder, who had joined the Polish Army, and for a fleeting moment it dawned on him that they could meet in battle. But there was a war to fight, and Siegfried moved on.

On Christmas Eve, 1941, Siegfried was in the trenches of the front lines during the Christmas truce. It was important for Siegfried, a captain, to be with his men at that time. One of his men had set up a listening device in the no-man's-land between his own position and the Russian Army. The ground was frozen, and acted as a wire for transmitting sound. What he heard from the enemy Russian soldiers startled him.

"Maybe the pacifist in me was born at that moment," notes Siegfried. "I heard the Russian soldiers singing the same Christmas songs that we sang in Germany. This kept coming back to me after the war—they were singing the same Christmas songs!"

Siegfried was a Christian before the war had ever started. The Bible was his steady companion. He shared his faith freely during the war. He prayed frequently for safety and survival, but never for victory.

In August of 1945, Siegfried was released and reunited with his family, who had survived the war. He maintained a farm management job until the Spring of 1951, when his family emigrated to Canada. The area where he had lived before the war had become part of Poland. He lost all his possessions and lands, and left with only a small amount of clothing and personal documents.

It was a difficult time, emotionally, for Siegfried. The reality of defeat made him question the value of the past. "People on the winning side seldom review. They are the heroes. If you are on the losing side, the victors look at you as if you were a criminal. I asked myself many times, 'What actually is Jesus expecting of me?' I thought I had followed him, but I had obeyed the State. We had on our belt buckles, 'God with us.' But that was a lie. The State's armies used Christianity for their own purpose. This was true in Germany, and this was true in the United States when the American military chaplain blessed the crew of bomber pilots going to Hiroshima."

During the war, Siegfried did not entertain thoughts about its justification. He thought only of obedience to the government and survival. Siegfried did not harbor anger or hate toward the enemy.

"The process of moving to a Christian pacifist position was a slow one," notes Siegfried. "For a short time, the stigma of being a German soldier in Canada was difficult, and increased my desire to isolate myself.

"I met many Mennonite church leaders in Canada who condemned the position I had taken in my past. They were not willing, and did not try to understand me. It was contacts with friends who attempted to understand me, that led me to a new understanding of Jesus' teachings about loving the enemy.

"The teaching of Jesus in Matthew 5:44 to love your enemies is as important as the new birth. People will always find justification for war, but we must teach against it categorically. There are many reasons for this justification of war, including political (from either side) and moral, but I do not believe there is a justification in the name of Christ."[2]

They Just Accepted Me

In 1968 Joe Blumber was a helicopter mechanic on duty with the U.S. military in South Vietnam. In 1985 Joe declined the military-related work assigned to him by his boss. The story of Joe's transformation includes the friendship and patience of several Mennonite congregations in Virginia.

I grew up in Pennsylvania, so I knew about the Amish," recalls Joe. "But I got better acquainted with the Mennonites when I went to college. One of my best friends was a Mennonite, and my wife was a General Conference Mennonite.

"In spite of these contacts, I never heard the Mennonite teaching on war and peace clearly articulated. My wife's father had served in the Navy."

During his first several months in Vietnam, Joe's helicopter landing zone was frequently under attack. "People beside me were hit, and my equipment was hit, but I was never wounded," recalls Joe. "Despite these situations, I was never plagued with moral or ethical questions about combat. To me, military service was a duty. I didn't question it."

Joe's experience in Vietnam was significant, however, in helping him come to some new understandings about peace. "I got to know some of the Vietnamese people, perhaps better than some of the other soldiers. I didn't speak Vietnamese, but I had Vietnamese friends who actually discussed their feelings and confided in me. I was always puzzled by the logic of their thinking.

"We talked about the U.S. military presence, and the tremendous destruction which our army had caused. I asked my Vietnamese friends if they would be glad when the Americans left their country. They always insisted that they were glad we were there, and that they would not want us to leave. But whenever I asked them about their support for Vietnamese leaders, they almost always said that they considered Ho Chi Minh (a North Vietnamese leader and the "enemy" of South Vietnam) to be their leader. I could never understand this, and began to wonder why our military was there."

Upon his return from Vietnam, Joe was assigned to the Newport News area, and once again came into contact with Mennonites. One of these contacts came through Project Transition, a military program designed to help combat veterans readjust to civilian life. This program placed combat veterans into civilian work settings before they actually left military service. Joe was assigned to work for Levi Weber, a local Mennonite building contractor.

Through his work with Levi Weber, Joe met the Longacre family. "They practically adopted me into their family," recalls Joe. "They just accepted me with my military background." The Longacres had been working on the construction of the Huntingdon Mennonite Church facility, and Joe and his family began attending church there. Among these people I saw a consistency which I hadn't seen before. Through their lives, I came to accept Jesus as my Lord.

"This was very different from what I had observed in the peace movement when I came back from Vietnam. In the peace movement, I saw people who had gone to Canada, and people who talked a lot about peace, but were willing to tear down or destroy everything."

Joe was invited to participate in an inquirer's class at the Huntington Mennonite Church. This was not a membership class, but a place where he could go and ask any questions that were on his mind. "It was nice, because they didn't make a fool out of me. Lloyd Weaver was the pastor at the time. If he didn't have the answer, he would do a bit of study and bring back a response the following week. At first I asked antagonistic questions, just to see what the response would be. Lloyd was always very patient with me and respectful of my questions. That really impressed me.

"In church, peace was linked to Christ in a way I had never thought about before. I never knew there was an alternative to war. I think many Christians are led into participating in wars just because they have never understood that there is an alternative.

"As I reflect back on my Vietnam experience, I feel real regret if I have harmed anyone. Since many of the combat situations occurred in the dark, it's hard to know the results of what I did. But I have repented, found forgiveness, and resolved never to take part in anything like that again."

In 1985 Joe's new understanding of Christ's way of peace and reconciliation was put to the test in an interesting way. "I worked for a construction company which did a lot of military work. My boss was patriotic. He always flew the flag. One day he announced that I would be assigned to build an ammunition bunker at the Naval Weapons Station. I went home that evening knowing that this wasn't going to happen. I called my pastor. He was very supportive and said the church would stand behind my decision.

"The next morning I went back to work, knowing that I would likely lose my job. I explained that my faith and understanding of the Lord's will would not allow me to build an ammunition bunker. To my surprise, my boss was very understanding. He said that he respected my opinion, and that he also respected the Mennonites who have a long and positive history in the community. He really didn't have other work to assign me to right away, but made work for me for about a month and a half until other work became available.

"Jesus' answer to the question, 'Who is my neighbor?' is central to my understanding of peace. The neighbor was always someone whom you had to cross a human dividing line to love. All of us need to put that into practice in our own lives.

"I want our church to be a place where anyone can come and hear the full Gospel. Persons who are currently in the military attend our church now. I want them to feel welcome and comfortable here. Here they can learn that Christ's way is the way of peace."

A Final Word

This book has brought together some of the wonderful stories from our faith family through the years and around the world. The stories reflect our sincere belief that peace with God means seeking a life of peace with others in the midst of a world which is often cruel and violent.

Central to this conviction is the example of Christ who taught us to love our enemies, and to pray for those who would mistreat or harm us. Many in our faith tradition have said no to war. For some, this has meant refusing military service. Others have also refused to pay taxes for war, or have withheld their labor from making weapons for war.

In recent years we have been challenged anew by the call to peacemaking in all areas of life. We have much to learn about peacemaking as it applies to:
- domestic violence and sexual abuse
- conflict in our churches
- unwanted pregnancies and abortion
- lawsuits and conflict in public life
- violence on the street
- cross-cultural relationships and racism
- lifestyles which withhold resources from the poor
- public witness

The stories in this book are filled with inspiration and courage from people who have been touched by a vision of peace and reconciliation for our world. We hope their presentation here can help inspire a new generation of peacemakers in the Spirit of Christ.

Acknowledgments

We have many people to thank. We are deeply indebted to all whose experiences fill the pages of this book. They have shared with honesty and humility from the depths of their experiences. Our lives have been immeasurably enriched through our conversations and correspondence.

We are grateful to our publishers for nudging us to begin this writing project. Their vision, practical help, and extraordinary patience sustained us as we brought the project to completion.

We are thankful to Mennonite Central Committee, for providing us with some release time from our normal duties to get this project "over the hump." In addition, many MCC and Mennonite mission agency workers, both in the U.S. and abroad, cheerfully helped us with interviewing, research and translation.

In particular, we would like to thank the following people who are not mentioned elsewhere: Daniel Erdman, Linda Shelley, Luke Schrock-Hurst, Doreen Harms, Daryl Yoder-Bontrager, Phil Stoltzfus, Harold Bergey, and Ann Hershberger.

We are grateful to Wayne Nisly and Keith Nisly who patiently and expertly guided us into a happy relationship with our computer.

We also want to thank our children, Beth Anne and Rachel Marie, who had to wonder for four long years when we were going to finally finish "the book." For them, and for all the children of the world, we wish a world where peace and life are honored. Until then, we pray that God will grant us courage and hope for the difficult and joyful task of peacemaking.

Titus Peachey
Linda Gehman Peachey

Notes

The Man Who Would Not Shoot (page 5):

1. Sharon Klingelsmith, comp., "Virginia Mennonites During the Civil War Era," *Mennonite Historical Bulletin*, 35 (January 74): p. 2.

2. Peter S. Hartman, *Reminiscences of the Civil War* Lancaster, PA: Eastern Mennonite Associated Libraries and Archives, 1964): pp. 10-11.

3. Adapted from L. J. Heatwole, "Brother Christian Good, Whose Gun Was 'Out of Order'," *Mennonite Historical Bulletin* 33 (July, 1972): p. 3.

At the beginning of his letter (dated Dec. 11, 1918), Heatwole explains that, "In regard to Brother Christian Good's experiences and trials in time of the Civil War, I am almost sure that he never left any account of them in writing, but I have heard the story related again and again by himself and younger brothers; besides I have a distinct recollection of the time when these incidents occurred."

Brackets for Turret Guns (page 7):

1. Richard Ross, letter dated in during fall of 1987.

Friday Will Be Peace Day (page 12):

1. From "Peace by Piece," a collection of teachers' experiences during the Gulf War, published by the Commission on Education of the General Conference Mennonite Church, Spring 1991.

Bombies and Armed Escorts (page 14):

1. The article "Cluster Bomb Has Programmable Option" appeared in *Aviation Week and Space Technology* on September 30, 1985.

Building Bridges, Building Hope (page 18):

1. Compiled and adapted from:
—Leon and LouAnn Ressler, Eastern Mennonite Board of Missions missionaries in Kenya (1980-1985), script of slide presentation and interview with authors, February 8, 1991.
—Carl E. Hansen (Eastern Mennonite Board of Missions missionary in Kenya since 1985), "Of Victims, Evangelists and Cattle Thieves," given to authors as an unpublished article.

Christ or Country (page 21):

1. Adapted from J. Georg Ewert, "Christ or Country?" *The Plough* 4 (May, 1984): pp. 6-10.

Inviting the IRS to Dinner (page 28):

1. *What Belongs to Caesar?* by Donald D. Kaufman is published by Herald Press (Scottdale, PA, 1969).

2. Compiled and adapted from:
—Ron Flickinger, "Interview With Paul and Loretta Leatherman," *Gospel Herald* (April 29, 1980): pp. 350-352.
—Paul Leatherman, interview and correspondence with authors, August 10, 1988.
—Paul Leatherman, "COs and Income Tax Time," *The Mennonite: the Magazine of the General Conference Mennonite Church* (March 10, 1981): p. 161.

I Have No Enemies (page 32):

1. Compiled and adapted from Thieleman J. van Braght, *Martyrs Mirror* (Scottdale, Pennsylvania: Herald Press, 1975): p. 962.

Slacker, Buy Liberty Bonds (page 38):

1. Joseph Boll, testimony at Hernley's Mennonite Church, Manheim, Pennsylvania, June 25, 1972.

On the Brink of Calamity (page 40):

1. David W. Shenk, *Peace and Reconciliation in Africa* (Nairobi, Kenya: Uzima Press Limited, 1983): pp. 166-167.

2. Adapted from Levi O. Keidel, *War to be One* (Grand Rapids, Michigan: Zondervan Publishing House, 1977): pp. 119-123.

I Would Like to Keep My Beliefs (page 43):

1. Adapted from Nicholas Stoltzfus, comp., "The Trying Experience of Rudy Yoder," *Nonresistance Put to Test* (Aylmer, ONT: Amish Publishing Service): pp. 7-24.

No Taxes for Vengeance (page 45):

1. Compiled and adapted from *The Chronicle of the Hutterian Brethren, Vol. 1*, trans. and ed. by the Hutterian Brethren (Rifton, NY: Plough Publishing House, 1987): pp. 81, 478, 512-514, 560-561, 670.

Understanding the Arab World (page 54):

1. Christian Peacemaker Teams promotes active, nonviolent peacemaking, and is sponsored by the Mennonite, Brethren in Christ and Church of the Brethren denominations.

Your Honor, I Will Not Be a Soldier (page 65):

1. William Janzen and Frances Greaser, *Sam Martin Went to Prison: The Story of Conscientious Objection and Canadian Military Service* (Hillsboro, Kansas: Mennonite Central Committee Canada and Kindred Press, 1990).

Legitimate Self-Defense (page 68):

1. Adapted from Bernhard J. Dick, "Something About the *Selbstschutz* of the Mennonites in South Russia, July, 1918-March, 1919," trans. and ed. by Harry Loewen and Al Reimer, University of Winnipeg,

Journal of Mennonite Studies 4 (1986): pp. 135-142.

I Don't Know Who's Going to Hire You! (page 77):
1. Albert N. Keim, *The CPS Story: An Illustrated History of Civilian Public Service* (Intercourse, Pennsylvania: Good Books, 1990): pp. 40, 81.
2. William Janzen and Frances Greaser, *Sam Martin Went to Prison: The Story of Conscientious Objection and Canadian Military Service* (Hillsboro, Kansas: Mennonite Central Committee Canada and Kindred Press, 1990): p. 58.
3. Adapted from Mervin J. Hostetler, "A Time to Remember: Civilian Public Service" *Christian Living* (May 1971): pp. 7-9.

Preaching to the Soldiers (page 80):
1. *The Politics of Jesus* by John Howard Yoder is published by William B. Eerdmans Publishing Co. (Grand Rapids, 1972).

Entering Samaria (page 83):
1. André Gingerich Stoner, *Entering Samaria*, Occasional Paper No. 12 (Akron, PA: Mennonite Central Committee, 1990).

An Individual Witness (page 85):
1. Keisuke Matsumoto, letters October 31, 1990 and May 15, 1991.

Getting A "Valve Job" from the U.S. Military (page 90):
1. Vietnam Christian Services is a relief agency which combined the efforts of Mennonite Central Committee, Church World Service and Lutheran World Relief.

Sermons on the Street (page 95):
1. Joan Gerig, interview with Titus Peachey and Phil Stoltzfus.

How Eve Yoder Triumphed in Defeat (page 99):
1. Compiled and adapted from:
--Richard K. MacMaster with Samuel L. Horst and Robert F. Ulle, *Conscience in Crisis: Mennonites and other Peace Churches in America, 1739-1789--Interpretation and Documents* (Scottdale, Pennsylvania: Herald Press, 1979): pp. 395-397, 441-442.
--Richard K. MacMaster, "How Eve Yoder Triumphed in Defeat," *Purpose* 9:5 (May 16, 1976): pp.1-3.

In a Peace Tradition (page 103):
1. Compiled and adapted from:
—Marion Keeney Preheim, "Lawrence Hart: Indian Chief in a Tradition of Peace," *Mennonite Reporter* 10 (November 24, 1980): p. 10.
—Information from Lawrence Hart, June 3, 1991.

The Spirit of Melchizedek on Dürerstreet (page 106):
1. Henk B. Kossen, letter dated October 20, 1990.

Recruited by the Contras (page 111):
1. Compiled from:
—MCC files, reports and letters dated 1986-1988.
—Conversations with Luke Schrock-Hurst, Mennonite Central Committee volunteer in Honduras (1986 to 1989).

Staying True to God's Call (page 113):
1. Adapted from *Hans Meier Tells His Story to a Friend* (Rifton, NY: Plough Publishing House, 1979): pp.1-2, 6-9, 14-15, 17-18, 23-26, 43-45.

I Know My Hands Are Clean (page 122):
1. Kobangu Thomas, as told to Levi O. Keidel, "I Preach With Happiness and Power Because I Did Not Use My Gun," *Congo Missionary Messenger* (April-June, 1963), reprinted in the *Canadian Mennonite* 12 (Jan. 12, 1964): p. 8.

Refusing a Military "Substitution" Tax (page 127):
1. *What Belongs to Caesar?* by Donald D. Kaufman is published Herald Press (Scottdale, PA, 1969); reprinted in German by Agape Verlag in 1984. German translation by Wolfgang Kraus.
2. Bruno Sägesser, from a letter dated Feb. 18, 1991.

Pressure on the Home Front (page 129):
1. Jonas S. Hartzler, *Mennonites in the World War or Nonresistance Under Test* (Scottdale: Mennonite Publishing House, 1922): pp. 162-163.
2. Manasses E. Bontrager, letter, *The Weekly Budget* (May 15, 1918): p. 3.

3. Bontrager/Miller section compiled and adapted from:
—Ted Joseph, "The United States Vs. H. Miller: The Strange Case of a Mennonite Editor Convicted of Violating the 1917 Espionage Act," *Mennonite Life* 30 (September, 1975): pp. 14-18.
—David Luthy, "The Arrest of an Amish Bishop—1918" *Family Life* (March, 1972): pp. 23-26.

Gunsmiths Who Quit Their Trade in Colonial America (page 137):
1. Adapted from Richard K. MacMaster, "Gunsmiths Who Quit Their Trade in Colonial America," *Purpose* 9:3 (March 7, 1976): pp.4-6.

A Peaceful Dutch Warrior (page 147):
1. "The Peaceful Dutch Warrior Goes Home," comp./trans. of Dutch newspaper articles and excerpts from the sermon given at the funeral of Jan Gleijsteen, Sr. *Mennonite Weekly Review* 66:17 (April 27, 1989): p. 6.

Struggling with Conscription in Colombia (page 150):
1. Compiled and adapted from:
—Peter Stucky, "Colombian Conscientious Objectors," *MCC Newsletter on the Americas* 3:1 (February, 1990): pp. 8-9.
—Peter Stucky, letter dated February 13, 1991 and fax dated May 28, 1991.

Scheduled for Execution (page 156):
1. C.Z. Mast, "Imprisonment of Amish in Revolutionary War," *Mennonite Historical Bulletin* 13 (January, 1952): pp. 6-7.

To Migrate or to Stay (page 157):
1. Gustav E. Reimer and G.R. Gaeddert, *Exiled by the Czar, Cornelius Jansen and the Great Mennonite Migration, 1874* (Newton, Kansas: Mennonite Publishing Office, 1956).
2. Adapted from Horst Mönnich, "Ich Verweigere den Kriegsdienst," *Gehört Gelesen* (February, 1974): pp. 61-81. Translated into English by Erich Lotz.

No Longer a Warrior (page 163):
1. *What Mennonites Believe* by J.C. Wenger is published by Herald Press (Scottdale, PA, 1977).
2. Carl E. Hansen, excerpted from a letter dated March 26, 1991, from Ogwedhi-Sigawa Project, Kenya.

The 1919 Petition (page 165):
1. Archives of the Mennonite Church, Goshen, Indiana: John N. Durr Collection (Hist. Mss. 1-203); and Mennonite General Conference, Peace Problems Committee (I-3-5.1).

From Military Service to Christian Nonresistance (page 172):
1. Adapted from Pierre Widmer, "From Military Service to Christian Nonresistance," *Gospel Herald* XLII (November 15, 1949): p. 1113, 1114, 1123, 1133.

Student Soldiers (page 178):
1. Ted Koontz, written reflections submitted in article form.

Nonresistance under Test (page 182):
1. Adapted from Nevin Bender and Emanuel Swartzendruber, *Nonresistance Under Test*, ed. by Richard Showalter (Irwin, OH: Conservative Mennonite Board of Missions and Charities, 1969).

We Are Ready to Serve as Substitutes (page 184):
1. Letter to the President of the United States, February 21, 1975. Printed as a letter to the editor, *The Mennonite: the Magazine of the General Conference Mennonite Church* (March 25, 1975): p. 196.

I Had to Review My Life (page 186):
1. Adapted from Ohno Michio, "War Tax Resistance in Japan," and letter dated January 20, 1989.

From the Flying Club to Civilian Public Service (page 198):
1. The Burke-Wadsworth Act was passed by Congress on September 16, 1940, and provided conscientious objectors the right to perform alternate service under civilian direction.

Dedicated to God (page 204):
1. R. S. Lemuel, interview with authors (July 1990) and letters dated December 31, 1990 and March 28, 1991.

Choosing Separation (page 214):
1. Compiled and adapted from:
—John C. Wenger, *Faithfully Geo. R., The Life and Thought of George R. Brunk, 1871-1938* (Harrisonburg, Virginia: Sword and Trumpet, Inc., 1978): pp. 21-23.
—Ethel Estella (Cooprider) Erb, *Through Tribulation to Crown of Life* (Hesston, Kansas: Record Printing Company, 1972): pp. 17-18.

I Could Have Killed My Cousin! (page 220):
1. Diether Goetz Lichdi, "The Story of Nazism and its Reception by German Mennonites," *Mennonite Life* (March 1981).
2. Nan Cressman, interview with Siegfried Bartel on MCC Ontario/Rogers Cable TV series, *Development Dialogue*.

Bibliography

Anabaptist History and Experience

Dyck, Cornelius J., ed. *An Introduction to Mennonite History.* Scottdale, PA: Herald Press, 1967.

Estep, William R. *The Anabaptist Story.* Nashville: Broadman Press, 1963.

Juhnke, James C. *Vision, Doctrine, War: Mennonite Identity and Organization in America, 1890-1930.* Scottdale, PA: Herald Press, 1989.

Keim, Albert N. *The CPS Story: An Illustrated History of Civilian Public Service.* Intercourse, PA: Good Books, 1990.

Kreider, Robert S. and Rachel Waltner Goossen. *When Good People Quarrel, Studies of Conflict Resolution.* Scottdale, PA: Herald Press, 1989.

Lichdi, Diether Guntz. *Mennonite World Handbook: Mennonites in Global Witness.* Carol Stream, ILL: Mennonite World Conference, 1990.

MacMaster, Richard K. *Land, Piety, Peoplehood: The Establishment of Mennonute Communities in America, 1683-1790.* Scottdale, PA: Herald Press, 1985.

Oyer, John S. and Robert S. Kreider. *Mirror of the Martyrs.* Intercourse, PA: Good Books, 1990.

Ruth-Heffelbower, Duane. *The Anabaptists Are Back: Making Peace in a Dangerous World.* Scottdale, PA: Herald Press, 1991.

Schlabach, Joetta Handrich. *Extending the Table: A World Community Cookbook.* Scottdale, PA: Herald Press, 1991.

Schlabach, Theron F. *Peace, Faith, Nation: Mennonites and Amish in Nineteenth Century America.* Scottdale, PA: Herald Press, 1988.

Peace Theology

Bainton, Roland. *Christian Attitudes Toward War and Peace.* Nashville: Abingdon, 1979.

Barrett, Lois. *The Way God Fights.* Scottdale, PA: Herald Press, 1987.

Barrett, Lois and John K. Stoner. *Letters to American Christians.* Scottdale, PA: Herald Press, 1989.

Drescher, John M. *Why I Am a Conscientious Objector.* Scottdale, PA: Herald Press, 1982.

Driver, John. *How Christians Made Peace with War.* Scottdale, PA: Herald Press, 1988.

Gwyn, Douglas, George Hunsinger, Eugene F. Roop and John Howard Yoder. *A Declaration on Peace: In God's People the World's Renewal Has Begun.* Scottdale, PA: Herald Press, 1991.

Kraybill, Donald B. *The Upside-Down Kingdom.* Scottdale, PA: Herald

Press, 1978.

McSorley, Richard J. *New Testament Basis of Peacemaking.* Scottdale, PA: Herald Press, 1985.

Yoder, John Howard. *The Politics of Jesus.* Grand Rapids: William B. Eerdmans Publishing Co., 1972.

Yoder, John Howard. *What Would You Do?* Scottdale, PA: Herald Press, 1983.

For Young Readers

Bauman, Elizabeth. *Coals of Fire.* Scottdale, PA: Herald Press, 1954.

Durrell, Ann and Marilyn Sachs, eds. *The Big Book for Peace.* New York: Dutton, 1990.

Dyck, Peter. *A Leap of Faith.* Scottdale, PA: Herald Press, 1990.

Lehn, Cornelia. *Peace Be With You.* Newton, KS: Faith and Life Press, 1982.

Steiner, Susan Clemmer. *Joining The Army That Sheds No Blood.* Scottdale, PA: Herald Press, 1982.

Index

Era Index

About the Authors

Titus and Linda Peachey serve as Co-Executive Secretaries for Mennonite Central Committee U.S. Peace Section. From 1981-1985, they served as directors of the Mennonite Central Committee relief and development program in Laos. Following their return to the U.S., they completed a study of military-related industries in Lancaster County, PA, titled World Peace Begins in Lancaster.

Titus Peachey was born in Grantsville, Maryland, and grew up in Plain City, Ohio. Following high school, he attended Rosedale Bible Institute and Eastern Mennonite College. From 1970-1973, Titus worked with the Mennonite church in Vietnam in an alternative service assignment. Titus graduated from Messiah College (Philadelphia campus) in 1977 with a degree in social work.

Linda Gehman grew up in southeastern Pennsylvania. In 1976, she graduated from Eastern Mennonite College with a Liberal Arts degree. Linda also studied at Associated Mennonite Biblical Seminaries and Lutheran Theological Seminary.

Titus and Linda have two daughters, Beth and Rachel. The family lives in Lancaster, Pennsylvania where they attend East Chestnut St. Mennonite Church.